My Kid's
Allergic to Everything
Dessert Cookbook

2nd edition

More than **100 Recipes**
for sweets & treats the
whole family will enjoy

MARY HARRIS & WILMA SELZER NACHSIN

CHICAGO
REVIEW
PRESS

D1411235

12/5/2011 Steve: You are an
inspiration and I
always learn so
much from you!
Enjoy This Book.
Love, Wilma

The Library of Congress has cataloged the earlier edition as follows:

Harris, Mary, 1953–.

My kid's allergic to everything dessert cookbook : sweets and treats the whole family will enjoy / Mary Harris and Wilma Nachsin; forewords by Rebecca Hoffman and Ida Mary S. Thoma.

p. cm.

Includes index.

ISBN 1-55652-303-3

1. Food allergy in children—-Diet therapy—-Recipes. 2. Desserts. I. Nachsin, Wilma, 1954–. II. Title.

RJ386.5.H37 1996

618.92'9750654--dc20

96-42047

CIP

Cover and interior design: Andrew J. Brozyna, www.ajbdesign.com
Cover photo: Kelly V. Brozyna

Published by Chicago Review Press, Incorporated
814 North Franklin Street
Chicago, Illinois 60610

ISBN 978-1-56976-533-3

Printed in the United States of America
5 4 3 2 1

CONTENTS

Dr. Rebecca S. Hoffman

When I was asked to write a foreword for this cookbook, I was pleased that another resource would be available to help my patients with food allergies. As we all know, adhering to special dietary constraints is very difficult, especially for children. This cookbook will hopefully broaden the menu choices available and provide some inspiration for developing many new recipe alternatives.

Food allergies manifest themselves in many ways: skin rashes such as eczema, nasal congestion, runny nose, frequent upper respiratory infections, hives, headaches, asthma, even life-threatening anaphylaxis.

Infants and very young children with allergies are often sensitive to foods, the most common sensitivities being egg, milk, wheat, soy, corn, and peanut. Children and adults may also have additional reactions to inhalant allergens, such as dust mites, molds, pollens, and animal dander.

One clue to look for when you think someone in your family has food allergies is an itchy, red, scaly skin rash, especially on the face or neck, or inside the elbows or behind the knees, that persists for weeks or months and may wax and wane over time. The rash may flare up after the individual eats a particular food, but sometimes this is too subtle to see. Another clinical sign of allergies in general is a cold that won't go away—runny, stuffy nose, cough, and fatigue. Asthma can also be a problem; this can be manifested by coughing, wheezing, shortness of breath, or a tight or congested chest. These symptoms occur either in a seasonal pattern or after exposure to a specific allergen such as a cat, exposure to a cold, or exercise.

Food allergy–induced asthma can also be part of the syndrome of anaphylaxis, which is a severe and sudden allergic reaction resulting in multiple symptoms such as hives, low blood pressure, difficulty breathing, and abdominal cramping and diarrhea. Food anaphylaxis is a life-threatening type of food allergy.

As you can see, food and inhalant allergies can show up in many different ways. The first step is to be suspicious of an allergy, either because of the nature of the symptoms or because of a family history of allergies. Next, you should look carefully at the possible allergens: foods, dust, dander, etc. Then work with your pediatrician, internist, family practitioner, or allergist to identify the problem areas. A good story of the symptoms, a complete physical examination, and a few selected tests should pinpoint the most likely offending allergens. Finally, working with your physician through elimination of foods and/or decreasing exposure to other environmental allergens should help toward eliminating chronic symptoms. For food allergies, elimination of the offending items is the only current proven method of symptom relief. Sometimes this is very difficult to accomplish, especially if the allergy is something as all-pervasive as wheat or egg. That is where this book offers hope and practical help.

The one good thing about food allergies is that, with strict avoidance, some children will eventually lose their sensitivity to a food. However, some food allergies do persist for life. Depending on the severity of the original reactions, repeat testing and even controlled food challenges can be done periodically to test for continued allergies.

Knowledge about the problem and perseverance in its treatment can usually control food and other allergies relatively well. As of yet, there is no cure for allergies, but with continued research, we may hope for medical breakthroughs.

Dr. Ida Mary S. Thoma

How wonderful for a child to have tasty snacks and fun foods without itching or wheezing! A happy, stress-free person (child or adult) is more apt to "outgrow" allergic manifestations. I wish that I had just such a cookbook as this one when I was dealing with food allergies in my family.

I have found through personal and family experiences that food allergies may cause a variety of symptoms. In our family, the hives and eczema (atopic dermatitis) suffered by one of our children was suspected to be caused by a food allergy. Our family doctor, S. C. Lavine, initially sent us to a dermatologist who chose to treat only the symptoms. Knowing of my background in immunology, Dr. Lavine then suggested that I track down the offending allergens, those foods that caused the dermatitis.

As eliminating one food at a time did not alleviate the symptoms, we knew that more than one food was involved. We then resorted to the following method, which I recommend be used under your doctor's guidance and with his or her approval.

Keep a food diary. After one week of listing all foods eaten, eliminate completely a selected food that has been eaten daily from the diet for four or five days. For example, if wheat is the test food, eliminate all wheat in any form. On the fourth or fifth day at breakfast (or at least eight hours after any other foods have been ingested), the test food only, in its purest form, should be eaten. For example, cream of wheat cereal, seasoned with salt only.

The person being tested should be observed for allergic reactions. If the food is indeed an allergen, within fifteen to thirty minutes one or more symptoms may occur: itching, a burning sensation, chills, a headache or an aura of bright lights or spots before the eyes, swelling of the nasal passages, wheezing, and perhaps, within an hour or so, diarrhea. If no symptoms occur, there is no strong allergy to the test food. We have found that if there is a strong allergic reaction, a dose of milk of magnesia will hasten the riddance of the allergen from the body.

To summarize the procedure that was successful for us:

1. The test food must be eaten daily for one week before the test.
2. The test food must then be eliminated completely from the diet for four or five days.
3. The test food alone must be given to the subject after he or she has fasted for at least eight hours. A single food is tested at one time. I allowed twenty-four hours or longer between tests, and tested only at breakfast.
4. The person must be observed carefully for at least forty to sixty minutes after ingesting the food.

In this way I found that our daughter was allergic to corn, oatmeal, and lamb (including lanolin in hand creams, as well as wool).

The food diary was extremely important. I used one page in a loose-leaf notebook to record for one week the foods eaten at each meal, as well as extra snacks and drinks ingested between meals. All changes, good or bad, in the general well-being of the allergic person were noted in the diary. The food diary also serves as a menu planner—useful in spacing foods to prevent the allergic person from picking up allergies. If the daily menu is varied and a particular food is given only every four or five days, there seems to be no increase in allergies. I think this is especially true of infants who show allergic reactions. Some of the more common allergens that it is wise to space are wheat and wheat products, corn and corn products, chocolate, oranges, oatmeal, eggs and egg products, and peanut butter. To avoid identified allergens, it is important to read all labels carefully on containers of prepared or processed foods, including canned and frozen foods, confections and snack foods, mixes, drinks, breads and cakes, salad dressing, and preserves.

In order to have a varied menu and still eliminate identified allergens, I found it necessary to prepare meals from simple, pure, basic ingredients, free of the substances causing the allergies, instead of the many foods we had been buying in processed forms. That is why I am so appreciative of this cookbook and all the possibilities for fun foods that it offers.

Acknowledgments

We wish to thank Dr. Rebecca S. Hoffman and Dr. Ida Mary S. Thoma for their invaluable assistance in clarifying the medical aspects of asthma and allergies and their symptoms, for discussing the efficacy of a food elimination diet, and for their encouragement in our search for alternate foods and recipes. We thank Dr. David G. Fisher for his careful editing of the chapters regarding yeast and the family and species of alternative flours; and for providing an excellent appendix for those who wish to pursue the definitive origins of their ingredients. Our heartfelt thanks to Cynthia Sherry and Michelle Schoob for all their hard work and painstaking attention to detail. Thanks to Jim Morris for coming up with the perfect title. And most important, we thank Aaron, Jacob, Josh, Jessie, Andy, and Jonathan, for their patience and their overworked tastebuds!

Introduction

Over a decade later, we look back and wonder how we ever got through those toddler and childhood years! One huge blessing we never realized would happen is that our children learned at a very early age how to say "NO!" to grandmas and grandpas with inappropriate treats, to classmates and uninformed teachers with snacks designed to create a runny nose, a wheezy cough, or even a trip to the emergency room. How much easier is it for our children now to say no to the deadly traps of teenhood.

This cookbook is designed for parents and caregivers who are coping with food allergies in their youngsters. You have picked up this book and started reading because you suspect, or your doctor has just told you, that your child is allergic to certain foods. You have noticed dark circles under your child's eyes, even after a good night's sleep; a wheezy sound when your child is breathing normally; a chronic stuffy or itchy nose; too many ear infections to be considered normal; dry, sensitive skin; a chronic cough when your child does not have a cold. As with any medical problem, you are urged to see your pediatrician if you haven't already; these symptoms are indications of allergies and asthma. However, if you feel your questions are not being addressed completely, *don't give up*! Continue talking to friends, reading health and nutrition literature, and looking for a doctor who will work with you and your child.

You, like us, want to be able to feed your child nutritious and healthy snacks that do not contain the foods he or she is allergic to. You want your child to be a normal part of the crowd, and to not feel singled out by what he or she eats.

Our children have been coping with allergies to cow's milk, wheat, corn, peanuts, almonds, white potatoes, chocolate, and egg albumin (egg white) for many years. We searched health food stores, libraries, and bookstores for alternative recipes for our children's main meals, snacks, and special occasions. Because so many of the allergy books and cookbooks we reviewed contained mostly main course recipes for adults with allergies, we wanted to create a cookbook of special desserts and snacks especially for children. It's heartbreaking to see your child at a birthday party unable to eat the cake because it was made with bleached, enriched flour made from wheat, eggs, and commercial baking powder. It's difficult for children to understand that when they go to another child's birthday party they can't have the ice cream because it was made with cow's milk, eggs, and corn syrup sweeteners. It's hard to explain that they can't eat the candy, cookies, or potato chips on grocery store shelves. We wanted to be able to provide as normal and healthy a diet as possible within their limitations.

We have created cake, pie, cookie, and dessert recipes for you to use on special occasions or just for fun. With our children's diet limitations, fun can be hard to find in the kitchen, and we believe childhood should be *fun*, not just healthy! We have also included a few breakfast ideas, modified for elimination diets.

In each recipe's list of ingredients, we have put the ingredient which works best first, for example, 1½ cups oat flour *or* spelt flour *or* amaranth flour. This means we have achieved the tastiest results with oat flour, but have also been successful using the other flours. If there is only one ingredient listed in a line, this means we have not found (or do not need) any alternatives. Please feel free to substitute ingredients you find exciting to work with or that your child especially likes. Our recipes show our favorite way to achieve each result, but certainly not the only way! Please be aware, however, that flour and grain substitutions don't always work out well; trial and error is the only way for you to determine how to make your own substitutions.

It can be difficult to buy healthful snacks while traveling. We found allowable snacks and ingredients not only at health food stores but also at local supermarkets, and we discuss those in chapter 11. Food allergies are often present with other allergies, asthma, and a wide variety of other health problems. We feel that the allergic reactions our children suffer from may be eased by eliminating many commercial chemical cleaners in our homes, by using products recommended by our doctors, and by using ecological pesticides and herbicides in our homes and gardens. While we are unaware of any medical studies to support this conclusion, we feel that the cleaner and safer the environment is, the easier it may be for children to cope with and outgrow their allergies, asthma, and other medical difficulties. Therefore, we have included some cleaning and pesticide tips, and addresses of organizations that can provide more detailed information than we are able to include here; you may find other resources in ecology handbooks and your local newspaper.

If you are interested in trying to keep your home and garden as chemical-free as possible, we have also included sources for further information, and suppliers for gardening and cleaning products.

We also included a list of cookbooks that we found to be useful as starting points in our search for allergen-free recipes. We realize that alternative ingredients for these recipes may be difficult to find in some areas, so we have included Web sites for mail-order products. We have tried to verify that the manufacturers listed in the resources chapter can provide mail-order ingredients to individual consumers at a reasonable cost, and that they can provide sufficient proof of organic certification to the consumer. You may already have sources for special ingredients: if they are different from the ones listed here we would love to hear about them! Support organizations are also included if you would like to seek further information about your child's specific allergy, want to investigate further the possibility of creating a cleaner environment, or just want someone to talk with.

The inclusion of brand-name products, organizations, and manufacturers is not an endorsement of them by us, but rather a guide for you to use in searching out healthy alternative products.

This cookbook is not intended to take the place of medical diagnosis or a nutritionist's services. It is intended only as a guide and resource for alternative ingredients and recipes. The publishers, authors, and contributors take no responsibility for this book's use as a substitute for qualified medical and nutritional diagnoses or for a consumer's unhappiness with a particular product.

We have accepted no remuneration in any form from any of the resources, manufacturers, and companies mentioned herein.

Know Your Flours and Their Alter Egos

Using alternative flours can be very confusing and scary. We live in a world full of pre-packaged box mixes for pancakes, cakes, and muffins—when we were faced with using alternative flours and ingredients, we were thrown for a loop! What can be used in place of bleached, enriched flour made from wheat for a birthday cake? After the initial panic died down, we realized that there are many flours made from grains and seeds that are just as easy to use as wheat, but the slightly different qualities (such as lower or absent gluten content) made finding the right proportions difficult. We explored many helpful resources, such as the University of Wisconsin's and University of Illinois's Extension Offices, diet books, and health food stores' employees, but in the long run the best teacher was experience. The charts in this chapter provide general information about using and combining these flours. However, certain flours work better than others when preparing a variety of baked goods. For your convenience, we have provided specific combination charts listing flours that work best for each category of baked goods that appear in this book. In each recipe's list of ingredients, we have put the ingredient which works best first, for example, oat flour *or* spelt flour *or* amaranth flour. This means we have achieved the tastiest results with oat flour, but have also been successful using the other flours. If there is only one ingredient listed in a line, this means we have not found (or do not need) any alternatives.

If you are dealing with a gluten allergy or intolerance, a yeast allergy, or celiac disease, there are a wide variety of resources available. We were fortunate in not having to deal with that severe medical problem, and our hearts are with you. There are some gluten-free recipes scattered throughout, such as Orange Snaps and Coconut Pancakes. Several resources are listed in chapter 13, such as www.landolakes.com for our favorite gluten-free flour mixture, which is suitable for substitution in many of your favorite recipes.

Gluten is the elastic component in many grains that reacts with liquids and yeast in the unbaked dough, expanding and forming a network of tiny expandable pockets that trap the carbon dioxide created during the leavening process, thus making the dough rise. Because wheat gluten is the stickiest and most elastic of all grain glutens, it sets the standard for ease of preparation and rising in breads and other baked goods.

Yeast is a fungus that produces the carbon dioxide during fermentation. It continually reproduces itself, feeding off gluten and sugars.

Gluten and yeast, singly or together, give the baked products their lighter texture and weight. Nongluten flours do not feed yeast at all; therefore rising must be forced by either adding a gluten flour to the nongluten flour in the recipe or by using a lot more of a different leavening agent, such as baking powder or baking soda, with an acidic ingredient.

Wheat and corn flour are used in many products under many different names. When a label indicates that modified food starch or a thickening agent has been used, you may assume that wheat or corn in some form has been added. Surprisingly, even some candies, such as licorice, use wheat flour as a thickener and stiffener. Other ingredient and trademark names that include wheat are: bran, bread crumbs, bulgur or burghol, couscous, cracker meal, durum, farina, many forms of "filler," gluten, graham, HVP (hydrolyzed vegetable protein), kamut, many types of modified food starch, MSG, orzo, pumpernickel, seitan, semolina, tabouleh, teff, some varieties of tempeh, wheat germ, some forms of yeast, Accent, and Postum. Corn and its other names are discussed in chapter 3. Family names are listed in the appendices.

Following are two lists of flours, gluten and nongluten. Almost all of our recipes require some gluten in order to obtain a well-baked and tasty dessert. Generally, you will get a better product using mostly gluten flours. If you are dealing with a gluten allergy or intolerance or celiac disease, the nongluten flour mixture from Land o' Lakes (see page 171) combined with guar gum is a wonderful substitute for gluten flours.

GLUTEN AND "STICKY" FLOURS

This list is of flours we use in baked goods. There is a variety of research regarding the gluten content of some of these flours. See our Resources chapter (page 169) for more information on how to find the right products for your home.

Amaranth

Made from the ground grains of the amaranth plant, it is in the Amaranth family (some Amaranth species do not produce edible seeds or grain). It ranges from an off-white to near-black color and has a bland flavor. It works well used as a coating and for baking, and the cooked whole grains may be used in salads. Other varieties of this family are grown for the green leaves, which may be cooked and eaten like spinach and are commonly known as pigweed. The flour is high in protein, calcium, fiber, and B vitamins.

Barley

Made from the ground grain of barley plants, it is in the Grass family. It is commonly used in the manufacture of malt. It has a white color and a mild flavor; it does not work well as a coating or for thickening gravies and sauces. It works well for baking, especially when mixed with a flour that bakes a heavier or denser product, such as rye or buckwheat.

Buckwheat (dark)

Made from the ground grain of the buckwheat plant. In spite of its name, it is not related to the Grass family, but belongs to the Buckwheat family, which includes rhubarb and sorrel. It has a medium brown color and a strong nutty flavor. It works well for a dark crispy coating, and when mixed with other flours it will give a solid texture to baked goods. It is not good for thickening sauces and gravies or for making a roux.

Buckwheat (light)

Made from the unroasted ground grain of the buckwheat plant. It belongs to the same family as the dark buckwheat and differs only in the preparation of the flour. The flavor can vary from mild to strong, and it has a light brown color. It is good for baking and for use as a coating, producing a medium-weight, dry product, but it is not good for thickening sauces and gravies or for making a roux.

Chickpea/Garbanzo Bean

Made from the dried, ground seeds of the chickpea plant, it is in the Bean family. It has a pale yellow color and a mild flavor. It is only fair for coating, but is excellent for thickening sauces and gravies. It can be used for baked goods but only when it is one quarter or less of the total flour used (e.g., ¼ cup chickpea flour with ¾ cup other flours).

Kamut

Made from ground grain of the kamut plant, it is a Triticum in the Grass family. *Kamut* is the Egyptian word for wheat; it is an ancient, nonhybridized form of wheat. It has an off-white color and a mild flavor. It is good when used for coating, but not for thickening sauces and gravies or for making a roux. It works very well for baking.

Millet

Made from the ground grain of the pearl millet plant, it is in the Grass family. It has an off-white color and a very mild flavor. It works for coating, although not as well as some other flours, and does not work well for thickening sauces and gravies or for making a roux. It is very good for baking, especially when mixed with other, more glutinous flours.

Oat

Made from the ground kernels of the oat plant, it is in the Grass family. It has an off-white to gray color and a mild flavor. It is very good for coating, for thickening sauces and gravies, and for making a roux. It is also excellent for baking, especially when mixed at a 3:1 ratio with another flour such as arrowroot or potato (e.g., ¾ cup oat flour with ¼ cup potato flour). *Note: rolled oats (heated and flattened kernels) are gluten-free.

Potato

Made from the cooked, dried, and ground tuber, it is in the Potato family. It has a white color and no flavor. Potato flour is not recommended for coating, but is very good for thickening sauces and gravies. In baking, it works best when mixed with another flour and can be used for up to half of the total flour used. Note that potato flour and potato starch are different and react in different ways when used. Do not substitute one for the other.

Quinoa

Made from the roasted, ground seeds of the quinoa plant, it is in the Goosefoot family. It has an ivory color and a bland flavor in very small amounts. The flavor and aroma are much stronger and yeasty when used as half or more of the total flour used. It does not work well for coating, thickening sauces and gravies, or for making a roux. It works extremely well for muffins or loaf cakes, especially when mixed with another gluten flour.

Rye

Made from the roasted, ground grain of the rye plant, it is in the Grass family. It has a very dark brown color and a strong, almost yeasty flavor. It works well as a coating but has too strong a flavor to use as a thickener for sauces and gravies or for making a roux. It works extremely well for breads and some cakes, such as carrot or zucchini, but not as well for cookies or more delicate baked goods.

Spelt

Made from ground grain of the spelt plant, it is in the nonhybridized Grass family. It has an ivory to white color and a bland taste. It works extremely well for baking but not as well for thickening or coating.

Teff

Made from the ground grain of the teff plant, it is a Triticum in the Grass family closely related to wheat. It has a medium to dark color, a coarse texture, and a mild flavor. It works well for baking but not as well for coating, for thickening sauces and gravies, or for making a roux.

NONGLUTEN FLOURS

Arrowroot

Made from the dried, ground West Indian arrowroot tuber, it is in the Marantaceae family. It has a snow-white color and no flavor. It can be used for a crispy, quick-cooking coating and works very well as a thickening agent. Small amounts may also be added to gluten flours for baking. In catalogs or on packaging, it may be called "flour," "powder," or "starch"; we have found no discernible differences, and in this book we call it arrowroot flour.

Coconut Flour

Made from fresh coconut meat that is dried and ground into a powder, it is in the Palm family. It has a snow-white color and a mild, slightly sweet flavor. It is good for baking. Because it is a nongluten flour, we recommend using additional leavening agents such as adding 1½ teaspoons Ener-G Egg Replacer powder mixed with 2 tablespoons water for each ounce of coconut flour used. It makes light, delicious pancakes and baked goods with a hint of coconut flavor.

Rice

Made from the dried, ground kernels of rice plants, it is in the Grass family. Flours milled from brown and from refined white rice are available; the colors range from white to light brown, and all have a mild flavor. It is not good for coating unless you are preparing tempura batter. It works best in baked goods when mixed with other flours and will impart a light, silky texture to the product.

Soy

Made from the roasted, dried, ground soybean, it is in the Bean family. It works well when used for coating, but not for thickening. It is good for baking used at a 1:3 ratio (e.g., ¼ cup soy flour with ¾ cup other flours). Make sure the flour you purchase has been made from already-roasted soybeans. Because soy has a higher oil content than other flours, you may wish to reduce the margarine/oil called for in a recipe by 1 teaspoon for each ¼ cup soy flour used. It will give a silky, almost puddinglike texture to your baked goods. Soy has also been determined to be a common allergen, so daily use is not recommended.

Tapioca

Made from the cooked, ground cassava root, it is from the Spurge family. Depending on the recipe, it may be helpful to dissolve the tapioca pearls in hot or cold water before using; see container for helpful hints. There are a variety of tapiocas available; small pearled quick-cooking tapioca was used in creating these recipes. Use 4 teaspoons tapioca for each 1 tablespoon cornstarch used in recipe.

"STICKY" FLOURS CHART

The more "sticky" a flour is, the more likely it is to behave like a gluten flour. Based on our experience and from information gleaned from many sources, we have developed the following list of flours and how they behave during the baking process.

MORE STICKY FLOURS	MEDIUM STICKY FLOURS	LEAST STICKY FLOURS	NONSTICKY FLOURS
buckwheat oat rye	amaranth kamut potato quinoa spelt teff	barley garbanzo millet	arrowroot coconut rice soy tapioca

GENERAL SUBSTITUTIONS AND AMOUNTS

The following charts describe general rules for substituting alternative flours for each 1 cup of bleached, enriched flour made from wheat, or 1 cup of whole wheat flour.

GENERAL FLOUR SUBSTITUTION CHART FOR ANY RECIPE

¼ cup amaranth flour and ¾ cup oat flour

1 cup to 1¼ cups rye flour

¼ to ½ cup buckwheat flour and ½ cup amaranth flour

⅝ to 1 cup potato flour

1 cup oat flour

½ to ⅔ cup barley flour and ½ cup oat flour

½ cup potato flour and ½ cup rye flour

⅝ cup rice flour and ⅓ cup rye flour

1 cup soy flour plus ¾ cup potato starch

GENERAL FLOUR SUBSTITUTION CHART FOR BAKED GOODS

DENSER BAKED GOODS (such as loaf cakes, pancakes, and muffins)	LIGHTER BAKED GOODS (such as white or yellow cakes, cupcakes, bar cookies, drop cookies, and piecrusts)
1 to 1¼ cup rye flour	¼ cup amaranth flour and ¾ cup oat flour
¼ to ½ cup buckwheat flour and ½ cup quinoa flour	½ cup oat flour and ½ cup millet flour
⅝ to 1 cup potato flour	½ cup oat flour and ½ cup spelt flour
½ cup potato flour and ½ cup rye flour	½ cup spelt flour and ½ cup amaranth flour
⅝ cup rice flour and ⅓ cup rye flour	¼ soy flour and ¾ cup oat flour
1 cup soy flour and ¾ cup potato starch	¼ cup coconut flour and ¾ cup oat *or* millet flour
½ cup coconut flour, ½ cup potato flour, and 2 teaspoons Ener-G Egg Replacer powder mixed thoroughly with 4 tablespoons water. Decrease liquid in recipe by 4 tablespoons.	

These proportions may not look like they would work, but due to the different families, classes, and characteristics of these grains, they do. Please note that all the alternative flours react differently with each other; you may want to experiment to find the best combinations for your own cooking and baking needs.

One helpful hint is to add a little more leavening (such as baking powder, baking soda, egg yolk, or egg substitute) if a coarser flour rather than a finer flour is used. A good rule of thumb is 2½ teaspoons of additional baking powder or an equivalent substitute for each 1 cup of coarse flour used.

Another suggestion is to let the batter or dough sit for a few minutes after all ingredients have been thoroughly mixed to allow the alternative flours to absorb any liquids; this helps the flours expand and rise a little better when baking.

As you become more proficient in mixing your favorite recipes and using your favorite flours you will develop a feel for when your dough is the right consistency for a well-baked product.

Appendix I lists the scientific and family names for the grains and flours referred to in this cookbook. Appendix II describes the different food families. A food family is a botanical classification of foods that are related first by the flower structure and second by genetic structure. A person with an allergy to one member of a specific food family may also be allergic to other foods in the same family. If your child is allergic to one food in a particular family, check with your doctor before using other members of that food family.

Following are more detailed charts that correspond to the recipe chapters for specific substitutions and combinations of alternative flours that we have discovered work best for cookies, cakes, fruit desserts, and crusts.

CAKE AND CUPCAKE FLOUR CHART (part 1)

These are suggested combinations of flours that work well for light tasting and less dense cakes. All combinations are for 1 cup.

NO means the flour alone or that combination of flours is not appropriate for a good cake.

OK means the flour may be used by itself and does not require another flour in addition to it.

ANY COMB. means any ratio of the two flours that adds up to 1 cup will make a good cake.

	AMARANTH	BARLEY
AMARANTH	OK	up to ¼ cup barley with ¾ cup or more amaranth
BARLEY	up to ¼ cup barley with ¾ cup or more amaranth	NO
CHICKPEA / GARBANZO	up to ¼ cup chickpea with ¾ cup or more amaranth	NO
MILLET	up to ¼ cup millet with ¾ cup or more amaranth	up to ¼ cup millet and up to ¼ cup barley with ½ cup *or* more oat *or* spelt
OAT	ANY COMB.	up to ½ cup barley with ½ cup or more oat
POTATO	up to ¼ cup potato with ¾ cup or more amaranth	up to ¼ cup potato and up to ¼ cup barley with ½ cup or more oat *or* spelt
QUINOA	ANY COMB.	up to ⅓ cup barley with ⅔ cup or more quinoa
RICE	up to ¼ cup rice with ¾ cup or more amaranth	up to ¼ cup rice and up to ¼ cup barley with ½ cup or more quinoa, oat, *or* spelt
SOY	up to ⅓ cup soy with ⅔ cup or more amaranth	up to ¼ cup soy and up to ¼ cup barley with ½ cup or more quinoa, oat, *or* spelt
SPELT	ANY COMB.	up to ½ cup barley with ½ cup or more spelt

My Kid's **Allergic to Everything** *Dessert Cookbook*

	CHICKPEA / GARBANZO	MILLET	OAT
AMARANTH	up to ¼ cup chickpea with ¾ cup or more amaranth	up to ¼ cup millet with ¾ cup or more amaranth	ANY COMB.
BARLEY	NO	up to ¼ cup barley and up to ½ cup millet with ½ cup or more oat *or* spelt	up to ½ cup barley with ½ cup or more oat
CHICKPEA / GARBANZO	NO	up to ¼ cup chickpea and up to ¼ cup millet with ½ cup or more oat *or* spelt	up to ½ cup chickpea with ½ cup or more oat
MILLET	up to ¼ cup millet and up to ¼ cup chickpea with ½ cup or more oat *or* spelt	NO	up to ½ cup millet with ½ cup or more oat
OAT	up to ½ cup chickpea with ½ cup or more oat	up to ½ cup millet with ½ cup or more oat	OK
POTATO	NO	up to ¼ cup potato and up to ¼ cup millet with ½ cup or more oat *or* spelt	up to ¼ cup potato with ¾ cup or more oat
QUINOA	up to ⅓ cup chickpea with ⅔ cup or more quinoa	up to ½ cup millet with ½ cup or more quinoa	ANY COMB.
RICE	up to ¼ cup rice and up to ¼ cup chickpea with ½ cup or more quinoa, oat, *or* spelt	up to ¼ cup rice and up to ¼ cup millet with ½ cup or more quinoa, oat, *or* spelt	up to ⅓ cup rice with ⅔ cup or more oat
SOY	up to ¼ cup soy and up to ¼ cup chickpea with ½ cup or more quinoa, oat, *or* spelt	up to ¼ cup soy and up to ¼ cup millet with ½ cup or more quinoa, oat, *or* spelt	up to ⅓ cup soy with ⅔ cup or more oat
SPELT	up to ½ cup chickpea with ½ cup or more spelt	up to ½ cup millet with ½ cup or more spelt	ANY COMB.

CAKE AND CUPCAKE FLOUR CHART (part 2)

These are suggested combinations of flours that work well for light tasting and less dense cakes. All combinations are for 1 cup.

NO means the flour alone or that combination of flours is not appropriate for a good cake.

OK means the flour may be used by itself and does not require another flour in addition to it.

ANY COMB. means any ratio of the two flours that adds up to 1 cup will make a good cake.

	POTATO	QUINOA
AMARANTH	up to ¼ cup potato with ¾ cup or more amaranth	ANY COMB.
BARLEY	up to ¼ cup potato and up to ¼ cup barley with ½ cup or more quinoa, oat, *or* spelt	up to ⅓ cup barley with ⅔ cup or more quinoa
CHICKPEA / GARBANZO	NO	up to ⅓ cup chickpea with ⅔ cup or more quinoa
MILLET	up to ¼ cup potato and up to ¼ cup millet with ½ cup or more quinoa, oat, *or* spelt	up to ½ cup millet with ½ cup or more quinoa
OAT	up to ¼ cup potato with ¾ cup or more oat	ANY COMB.
POTATO	NO	up to ¼ cup potato with ¾ cup or more quinoa
QUINOA	up to ¼ cup potato with ¾ cup or more quinoa	OK
RICE	up to ¼ cup potato and up to ¼ cup rice with ½ cup or more quinoa, oat, *or* spelt	up to ¼ cup rice with ¾ cup or more quinoa
SOY	up to ¼ cup potato and up to ¼ cup soy with ½ cup or more quinoa, oat, *or* spelt	up to ¼ cup soy with ¾ cup or more quinoa
SPELT	up to ¼ cup potato with ¾ cup or more spelt	ANY COMB.

	RICE	SOY	SPELT
AMARANTH	up to ¼ cup rice with ¾ cup or more amaranth	up to ⅓ cup soy with ⅔ cup or more amaranth	ANY COMB.
BARLEY	up to ¼ cup rice and up to ¼ cup barley with ½ cup or more quinoa, oat, *or* spelt	up to ¼ cup soy and up to ¼ cup barley with ½ cup or more quinoa, oat, *or* spelt	up to ½ cup barley with ½ cup or more spelt
CHICKPEA / GARBANZO	up to ¼ cup rice and up to ¼ cup chickpea with ½ cup or more quinoa, oat, *or* spelt	up to ¼ cup soy and up to ¼ cup chickpea with ½ cup or more quinoa, oat, *or* spelt	up to ½ cup chickpea with ½ cup or more spelt
MILLET	up to ¼ cup rice and up to ¼ cup millet with ½ cup or more quinoa, oat, *or* spelt	up to ¼ cup soy and up to ¼ cup millet with ½ cup or more quinoa, oat, *or* spelt	up to ½ cup millet with ½ cup or more spelt
OAT	up to ⅓ cup rice with ⅔ cup or more oat	up to ⅓ cup soy with ⅔ cup or more oat	ANY COMB.
POTATO	up to ¼ cup rice and up to ¼ cup potato with ½ cup or more quinoa, oat, *or* spelt	up to ¼ cup soy and up to ¼ cup potato with ½ cup or more quinoa, oat, *or* spelt	up to ¼ cup potato with ¾ cup or more spelt
QUINOA	up to ¼ cup rice with ¾ cup or more quinoa	up to ¼ cup soy with ¾ cup or more quinoa	ANY COMB.
RICE	NO	up to ¼ cup soy and up to ¼ cup rice with ½ cup or more quinoa, oat, *or* spelt	up to ¼ cup rice with ¾ cup or more spelt
SOY	up to ¼ cup rice and up to ¼ cup soy with ½ cup or more quinoa, oat, *or* spelt	NO	up to ¼ cup soy with ¾ cup or more spelt
SPELT	up to ¼ cup rice with ¾ cup or more spelt	up to ¼ cup soy with ¾ cup or more spelt	OK

PIE CRUST AND TOPPING FLOUR CHART

These are suggested combinations of flours that work well for dough pie crusts or toppings.

All combinations are for a total of 1½ cups flour, which is a sufficient amount for both 9-inch crust and toppings.

NO means the flour alone or that combination of flours is not appropriate for a good pie crust.

OK means the flour may be used by itself and does not require another flour in addition to it.

ANY COMB. means any ratio of the two flours which adds up to 1½ cups will make a good pie crust.

	AMARANTH	BARLEY	OAT	POTATO	QUINOA	SPELT
AMARANTH	NO	NO	ANY COMB.	1¼ cup amaranth with ¼ cup potato	ANY COMB.	ANY COMB.
BARLEY	NO	NO	½ cup barley with 1 cup oat	NO	½ cup barley with 1 cup quinoa	½ cup barley with 1 cup spelt
OAT	ANY COMB.	1 cup oat with ½ cup barley	OK	NO	ANY COMB.	ANY COMB.
POTATO	¼ cup potato with 1¼ cup amaranth	NO	NO	NO	¼ cup potato with 1¼ cup quinoa	¼ cup potato with 1¼ cup spelt
QUINOA	ANY COMB.	1 cup quinoa with ½ cup barley	ANY COMB.	1¼ cup quinoa with ¼ cup potato	OK	ANY COMB.
SPELT	ANY COMB.	1 cup spelt with ½ cup barley	ANY COMB.	1¼ cup spelt with ¼ cup potato	ANY COMB.	OK

BERRY AND FRUIT DESSERT DOUGH FLOUR CHART

All combinations are for 1 cup.

NO means the flour alone or that combination of flours is not appropriate for a good dough topping.

OK means the flour may be used by itself and does not require another flour in addition to it.

ANY COMB. means any ratio of the two flours that adds up to 1 cup will make a good dough topping.

	AMARANTH	BARLEY	CHICKPEA/ GARBANZO	MILLET
AMARANTH	OK	⅓ cup barley with ⅔ cup amaranth	up to ⅓ cup chickpea with ⅔ cup or more amaranth	⅓ cup millet with ⅔ cup amaranth
BARLEY	⅓ cup barley with ⅔ cup amaranth	NO	NO	ANY COMB.
CHICKPEA / GARBANZO	up to ⅓ cup chickpea with ⅔ cup or more amaranth	NO	NO	NO
MILLET	⅓ cup millet with ⅔ cup amaranth	ANY COMB.	NO	NO
OAT	ANY COMB.	ANY COMB.	up to ¼ cup chickpea with ¾ cup or more oat	ANY COMB.
POTATO	up to ¼ cup potato with ¾ cup or more amaranth	NO	NO	NO
QUINOA	ANY COMB.	¼ cup barley with ¾ cup quinoa	NO	NO
RICE	NO	NO	NO	NO
SOY	NO	NO	NO	NO
SPELT	ANY COMB.	½ cup barley with ½ cup spelt	¼ cup chickpea with ¾ cup spelt	ANY COMB.

My Kid's *Allergic to Everything* Dessert Cookbook

	OAT	POTATO	QUINOA	RICE	SOY	SPELT
AMARANTH	ANY COMB.	up to ¼ cup potato with ¾ cup or more amaranth	ANY COMB.	NO	NO	ANY COMB.
BARLEY	ANY COMB.	NO	¼ cup barley with ¾ cup quinoa	NO	NO	½ cup barley with ½ cup spelt
CHICKPEA / GARBANZO	up to ¼ cup chickpea with ¾ cup or more oat	NO	NO	NO	NO	¼ cup chickpea with ¾ cup spelt
MILLET	ANY COMB.	NO	NO	NO	NO	ANY COMB.
OAT	OK	up to ¼ cup potato with ¾ cup or more oat	¼ cup quinoa with ¾ cup oat	¼ cup rice with ¾ cup oat	¼ cup soy with ¾ cup oat	ANY COMB.
POTATO	up to ¼ cup potato with ¾ cup or more oat	NO	NO	NO	NO	¼ cup potato with ¾ cup spelt
QUINOA	¼ cup quinoa with ¾ cup oat	NO	OK	NO	NO	ANY COMB.
RICE	¼ cup rice with ¾ cup oat	NO	NO	NO	NO	¼ cup rice with ¾ cup spelt
SOY	¼ cup soy with ¾ cup oat	NO	NO	NO	NO	¼ cup soy with ¾ cup spelt
SPELT	ANY COMB.	¼ cup potato with ¾ cup spelt	ANY COMB.	¼ cup rice with ¾ cup spelt	¼ cup soy with ¾ cup spelt	OK

COOKIE FLOUR CHART

These are suggested combinations of flours that work well for cookies. All combinations are for 1 cup.

NO means the flour alone or that combination of flours is not appropriate for a good cookie.

OK means the flour may be used by itself and does not require another flour in addition to it.

ANY COMB. means any ratio of the two flours that adds up to 1 cup will make a good cookie.

	AMARANTH	BARLEY	CHICKPEA/GARBANZO
AMARANTH	OK	¼ cup barley with ¾ cup amaranth	¼ cup chickpea with ¾ cup amaranth
BARLEY	¼ cup barley with ¾ cup amaranth	OK	¼ cup chickpea and ¼ cup barley with ½ cup quinoa, oat, *or* spelt
CHICKPEA / GARBANZO	up to ¼ cup chickpea with ¾ cup or more amaranth	¼ cup chickpea and ¼ cup barley with ½ cup or more quinoa, oat, *or* spelt	NO
MILLET	up to ¼ cup millet with ¾ cup or more amaranth	up to ¼ cup millet and up to ¼ cup barley with ½ cup or more quinoa, oat, *or* spelt	up to ¼ cup millet and up to ¼ cup chickpea with ½ cup or more quinoa, oat, *or* spelt
OAT	ANY COMB.	¼ cup barley with ¾ cup oat	up to ¼ cup chickpea with ¾ cup or more oat
QUINOA	ANY COMB.	¼ cup barley with ¾ cup quinoa	up to ¼ cup chickpea with ¾ cup or more quinoa
SPELT	ANY COMB.	¼ cup barley with ¾ cup spelt	up to ¼ cup chickpea with ¾ cup or more spelt

My Kid's *Allergic to Everything* Dessert Cookbook

	MILLET	OAT	QUINOA	SPELT
AMARANTH	up to ¼ cup millet with ¾ cup or more amaranth	ANY COMB.	ANY COMB.	ANY COMB.
BARLEY	up to ¼ cup millet and up to ¼ cup barley with ½ cup or more quinoa, oat, *or* spelt	¼ cup barley with ¾ cup oat	¼ cup barley with ¾ cup quinoa	¼ cup barley with ¾ cup spelt
CHICKPEA / GARBANZO	up to ¼ cup chickpea and up to ¼ cup millet with ½ cup or more quinoa, oat, *or* spelt	up to ¼ cup chickpea with ¾ cup or more oat	up to ¼ cup chickpea with ¾ cup or more quinoa	up to ¼ cup chickpea with ¾ cup or more spelt
MILLET	NO	up to ¼ cup millet with ¾ cup or more oat	up to ¼ cup millet with ¾ cup or more quinoa	up to ¼ cup millet with ¾ cup or more spelt
OAT	up to ¼ cup millet with ¾ cup or more oat	OK	ANY COMB.	ANY COMB.
QUINOA	up to ¼ cup millet with ¾ cup or more quinoa	ANY COMB.	OK	ANY COMB.
SPELT	up to ¼ cup millet with ¾ cup or more spelt	ANY COMB.	ANY COMB.	OK

Sweeteners: Nectars, Syrups, and Powders, Oh My!

Sweeteners are used to sweeten and/or add flavor to foods and baked goods. Many kinds of sweeteners are available in addition to granulated cane sugar. Fruit sweeteners come in many forms, including granulated, powdered, dried, pureed, juiced, juice concentrates, liquid, sauce, and mashed. Having a variety of sweeteners to choose from in your pantry will add interest and flavor variations to your foods. If you want to substitute one sweetener for another, the rule of thumb is to use dry sweetener for dry sugar and liquid sweetener for liquid sugar. Depending on the form of sweetener used the other liquids in your recipe may have to be reduced and/or the dry ingredients increased. We have not tried all of these sweeteners in our recipes. For equivalent substitutions follow package directions or experiment. See chapter 13 for mail-order sources for most of these items when they are not readily available at your local grocery or health food store.

Agave Nectar Syrup (light, medium, and amber)
A thick syrup that is produced by filtering and heating the sap of the agave plant, a succulent plant in the Agavaceae family. Also called agave syrup. Light agave has a mild flavor while the darker agave is more intense. Agave nectar is about 1½ times sweeter than granulated sugar. To substitute agave nectar for sugar in a recipe, use ⅔ cup agave nectar for 1 cup granulated sugar, and reduce the liquid in the recipe by ¼. Reduce the baking temperature by 25°F.

Agave Powder, also called Inulin Powder
A fine powder produced from the dried sap of the agave plant, a succulent plant in the Agavaceae family. Agave powder is almost as sweet as confectioners' or powdered sugar, and is a very good substitute. Use 1 cup agave powder for 1 cup granulated sugar.

Barley Malt
A thick syrup or powder made from barley grains, it has a flavor similar to molasses. It is in the Grass family and makes a good substitute for brown sugar. For 1 cup of granulated sugar, use 1½ cups barley malt syrup and reduce liquids by 1 to 2 tablespoons.

Beet Sugar

Made from the refined and dried syrup of the sugar beet. It is in the Goosefoot family. Use it in equivalent amounts to replace granulated sugar in the recipe.

Brown Sugar (light or dark)

Made from either granulated cane sugar (from the sugarcane stalks of the Grass family) or beet sugar with molasses (also from sugarcane stalks). Adds flavor and color. Use 1 cup firmly packed brown sugar for each cup of granulated sugar.

Cane Sugar

Made from liquid squeezed from the sugarcane stalks of the Grass family. It is dried and refined to make granulated sugar. It is the most common sweetener used in baked goods.

Coconut Sap Sugar or Palm sugar

It is in the Palm family. Produced by boiling and concentrating the nectar from the sap of the tropical coconut palm sugar blossoms, resulting in sugar blocks, a soft paste, or granulated crystals. Not quite as sweet as cane sugar. Follow package directions for substitution information.

Confectioners' Sugar or Powdered Sugar

Finely ground cane sugar. It comes from the Grass family. Normally used to provide a silky, smooth frosting or a less dense baked good. Commercial confectioners' sugars have added cornstarch to assure a dry and free-flowing product.

To make your own confectioners' sugar: Slowly pour granulated sugar ¼ cup at a time into the top opening of a blender or food processor already going on high speed. Empty blender or food processor after each ¼ cup is ground. A level ½ cup granulated sugar will yield a heaping ½ cup of confectioners' sugar. Use the amount called for in the recipe.

Corn Syrup Sweetener (light or dark)

Made from liquid squeezed from corn kernels. Commonly known as corn syrup, cerelose, dextrose, glucose, and Karo syrup; it is in the Grass family. It is a very inexpensive sweetener and is used extensively in commercial products such as sodas, breakfast cereals, cookies, and many other items. If this is an allergen, great care must be taken to avoid corn under its many names. If your recipe calls for corn syrup, for each 1 cup used you may substitute 1 cup granulated sugar melted over low heat with ¼ cup water.

Dates and Date Sugar

It is from the Palm family. Date sugar is made of dried ground dates. Date paste is made by processing fresh dates in a food processor or blender until the pasty texture is achieved. Date paste can be stored for months in your refrigerator. Use ⅔ cup date paste *or* 1 cup date sugar for each 1 cup of granulated sugar used in recipe.

Fructose

A sugar found in some vegetables, nearly all fruits, and honey. It is twice as sweet as granulated cane sugar and is available as a liquid, powder, or tablet. High fructose corn sweetener is used in many processed foods. See package ingredients to determine the source of the fructose. Follow package directions for substitution information.

Fruit Juices and Concentrates

Made from the juice of fruit that has been cooked at low temperature and reduced to a syrupy texture. Includes frozen juice concentrates that must be thawed before using. Use full strength (not diluted with water) to replace the liquid in the recipe; see chart, page 27. This adds both sweetness to the baked good and also the needed acidity for the leavening process. See package ingredients to determine the source of any added sweetener.

Fruit Purees and Whips

Can be purchased or made at home using a blender or food processor. Simply peel and pit larger fruits or seed berries and blend or process until smooth. For some berries, such as raspberries, put through a sieve or fine strainer to remove seeds before using. Commonly used fruits include apple, apricot, banana, date, fig, pear, plum, and prune. Fruit purees and whips can greatly improve the texture of many baked goods by helping to bind crumbly desserts. You can reduce the amount of the oil by the amount of fruit puree used.

Granulated Sugar

See cane *or* beet sugar.

Honey

Made by bees from the nectar of flowering plants. Honey is two and a half to five times sweeter than granulated sugar. Raw, unfiltered, locally produced honey is helpful for people with allergies: 2 tablespoons per day, taken any way you like, in the spring and in the fall will reduce the symptoms quite a bit. (Note that honey should not be consumed by children under the age of 18 months due to their inability to handle the bacteria that may be present in the honey.) Decrease the liquid called for in a recipe by ¼ cup for each 1 cup of honey. For example, if the recipe uses 1 cup allowable milk and 1 cup granulated cane sugar, use ¾ cup allowable milk and ¾ to 1 cup honey, to taste.

Maple Sugar and Syrup

Sap from trees in the Maple family is filtered and boiled down to a very sweet syrup and is a fine replacement for granulated cane sugar. Since many types of commercial maple syrup and "breakfast" syrups and some maple sugars contain corn sweeteners, be sure you are buying pure 100 percent maple syrup or maple sugar. Decrease the liquid called for by ¼ cup for each 1 cup of maple syrup. For example, if the recipe uses 1 cup allowable milk and 1 cup granulated cane sugar, use ¾ cup allowable milk and 1 cup maple syrup. Use an equivalent amount of maple sugar for the amount of granulated cane sugar used in the recipe.

Molasses

The syrupy residue left from the process that produces granulated sugar from sugar canes. It has a strong, sweet, but almost sulphuric taste that comes through clearly in baked goods. It is not recommended as the only substitute for cane sugar or other sweeteners when cooking or baking, but is tasty in many foods when used in combination with other sweeteners.

Rapadura

Organic unrefined cane sugar. *See* cane sugar.

Rice Sugar, Rice Syrup, Rice Powder

Produced from processed rice grains. Rice is from the Grass family. It has a light, smooth texture and a very mild flavor. It is available as a syrup or a powder. Use an equivalent amount of rice sugar for the amount of granulated sugar used in your recipe.

Stevia

It is a sweet herb from the Sunflower family. *Stevia rebaudiana* is available as a brownish or a white powder or as a liquid. It has a strong licorice-like taste and is a very concentrated sweetener, generally 10 times sweeter than sugar. Use it with other strong flavors like chocolate or carob or most fruits. You may want to stir it into the recipe's liquid for better distribution. Sometimes commercially packaged stevia is mixed with another sweetener so check the label for added ingredients and substitution amounts. Stevia may also be of concern to diabetics; check with your health care provider before using. Sugar to pure stevia conversions:

    1 cup sugar = 1 teaspoon powdered stevia

    1 cup sugar = 1 teaspoon liquid stevia

    1 tablespoon sugar = ¼ teaspoon stevia

When baking, for every 1 cup of sugar that is replaced by stevia, add ½ cup of fruit puree. Any puree with a flavor similar to the recipe will work. For example, use extra banana puree for the liquid or fat in a banana bread recipe. Fruit puree suggestions include:

- Apple sauce
- Apple butter
- Banana puree
- Canned unsweetened pumpkin

Sucanat

Unrefined sugar extracted from sugar cane. *See* cane sugar.

Turbinado

A by-product of the granulated sugar cane process. It is a less refined sugarcane sweetener, usually coarse in texture and with a molasseslike flavor. It may be used in equivalent amounts to replace granulated cane sugar.

Xylitol

Normally used as a powdered sweetener, such as in chewing gum. It occurs naturally and can be found in berries, fruit, vegetables, and trees. Commercial xylitol in the supermarket is highly processed and is either made from Chinese corn or from the birch tree;

if you cannot verify the source, it's best to avoid using it. It may be used in equivalent amounts to replace granulated sugar. If batter seems too dry, add liquid one teaspoon at a time until the texture seems right. Also, recently (2009) a veterinarian's group in Chicago released the information that xylitol is toxic for cats; store carefully.

Yacon Syrup

Produced from the roots of the yacon plant, it is a member of the Sunflower family. The syrup has a deep, rich flavor comparable to molasses or honey but is slightly sweeter. Decrease the liquid called for in the recipe by ¼ cup for each 1 cup of yacon syrup. For example, if the recipe uses 1 cup allowable milk and 1 cup granulated cane sugar, use ¾ cup allowable milk and ¾ to 1 cup yacon syrup, to taste.

SWEETENER SUBSTITUTION CHART

Substitution amounts are for 1 cup white granulated sugar.

It is easiest to substitute a liquid sweetener with another liquid sweetener and a dry sweetener with another dry sweetener. When you substitute a liquid sweetener for a dry one or vice versa, the recipe will need to be adjusted so the baked good has the right texture.

Generally, to replace 1 cup dry sweetener with 1 cup liquid sweetener, reduce another liquid by ¼ to ⅓ cup *or* add 4 to 5 tablespoons flour.

To replace 1 cup liquid sweetener with 1 cup dry sweetener, add ⅓ cup liquid.

SWEETENER	SUBSTITUTION AMOUNT	NOTES
Agave Nectar Syrup	⅔ cup	Reduce the liquid by ¼ cup and lower the baking temperature by 25°F
Agave Powder or Inulin	1 cup	If using the vanilla agave powder, you may want to decrease the amount of alcohol-free vanilla used in the recipe
Barley Malt	1½ cup	Reduce liquids by 1 to 2 tablespoons
Beet Sugar	1 cup	
Brown Sugar	1 cup firmly packed	
Cane Sugar	1 cup	
Coconut or Palm Sugar	1 cup	
Confectioners' Sugar	1 cup	
Date Paste	⅔ cup	
Date Sugar	1 cup	
Fructose	½ to ⅔ cup	See package ingredients for source of fructose
Fruit Juices Concentrates	½ cup	Use full strength and reduce the liquid in the recipe *or* add 2 to 3 tablespoons flour
Honey	¾ cup	Reduce liquid by ¼ cup
Maple Syrup	1 cup	Decrease the liquid called for by ¼ cup for each 1 cup of maple syrup
Molasses	½ to ¾ cup	Use in combination with other sweeteners due to strong taste
Rapadura	1 cup	
Rice Sugar or Syrup	1 cup	
Stevia	1 teaspoon	Add ½ cup of fruit puree per teaspoon of stevia used
Sucanat	1 cup	
Turbinado Sugar	1 cup	
Yacon Syrup	¾ to 1 cup	Reduce the liquid by ¼ cup

Taking Stock of Other Ingredients

Many of the products commonly used for baking and cooking regularly contain ingredients that may be allergens for your child. This chapter discusses the components of commonly available products and suggests substitutions and alternatives that work just as well. We have found that it is easiest to buy products from health food stores and manufacturers who can guarantee the purity of their ingredients. But if you do not have easy access to a health food store and need substitutions quickly, we hope this chapter will make your life easier. Check chapters 11 and 13 for suppliers who will send products to your home.

COMMON INGREDIENTS AND THEIR SUBSTITUTES

Baking Powder

Used as a leavening agent to help baked goods rise. Most baking powders have added cornstarch to keep the powder dry and free pouring. Many have albumin (egg whites) to assist the rising process. Substitute any of the following for each 1 teaspoon baking powder used in a recipe:

- ½ teaspoon cream of tartar and ½ teaspoon baking soda
- 1 teaspoon Featherweight, Hain, or Whole Foods' 365 generic brand baking powder or any brand that is cereal free (has no cornstarch)
- 1 teaspoon cream of tartar, 1 teaspoon bicarbonate of soda, and ½ teaspoon salt (if you are following a recipe that is not in this book, combine for each 1 cup flour used in the recipe)

Baking Soda

Sometimes used as a leavening agent to help baked goods rise, but not as commonly used as baking powder. Baking soda has no added ingredients, and may be used as it is. No substitutes are necessary.

Butter

Normally used to provide fats to assist baked goods in rising and to add a rich and full-bodied flavor. All cow's milk butters and blends and most margarines are based on cow's milk products. Use any one of the following substitutes in equivalent proportions to amounts used in recipes:

- applesauce: for 1 cup butter substitute ¾ cup to 1 cup applesauce
- coconut butter, coconut oil, coconut cream (preferably the thick waxy cream collected at the top of the can)
- flaxseed oil, canola oil, *or* other allowable mild-flavored oil
- goat's milk butter (see note under "cow's milk" [page 33] for important details)
- lard
- nondairy (uses no whey or lactose) non-corn oil margarine
- shortening (nondairy, non-corn, and/or vegan)
- tofu, soft regular (not firm or low fat) blended in blender or food processor

Carob

Carob is made from the roasted, ground, sticky pulp found in the seed pods of the Fabaceae carob tree; it is in the Bean family. It has a taste very similar to chocolate. Make sure, however, that the carob product has no added ingredients that are allergens.

Chocolate

While chocolate candy may have hidden additives, pure baking chocolate and pure cocoa may not be allergic substances for your child. Milk chocolate bars, such as Hershey's, do not have the egg-white gloss that is normally added to boxed candy for consumer eye appeal. Note, however, that white chocolate is derived from the coca bean. If your child has a chocolate allergy, you should check with your doctor before using white chocolate or any coca-bean derivative. Also most milk chocolates and some carob products use a dairy derivative and may also use a corn syrup sweetener. Be sure to check their ingredients list carefully. Any product with the word "pareve" or "parve" is guaranteed dairy free.

Substitute carob powder or carob chips for baking chocolate, cocoa, or chocolate chips in equivalent proportions to amounts used in recipes. Make sure that the carob substitute has no added ingredients that are allergens.

*My Kid's **Allergic to Everything** Dessert Cookbook*

Confectioners' Sugar

Finely ground cane sugar. It comes from the Grass family. Normally used to provide a silky, smooth frosting or a less dense baked good. Commercial confectioners' sugars have added cornstarch to assure a dry and free-flowing product. This is also sometimes called powdered sugar. An excellent substitute is agave inulin powder in equivalent proportions to amounts used in recipes.

To make your own confectioners' sugar see page 22.

Corn

It is in the Grass family. Some other names for corn products used in processed foods include: bran, caramel, cerelose, dextrose, fructose, germ meal, glucose, gluten meal, grits, hominy, HVP (hydrolyzed vegetable protein), Karo, maize, maltodextrin, masa harina, modified food starch, polenta, pozole, sucrose, and xanthan gum.

Note: cornhusks and corncobs may be used to create cardboard containers. Even containers that state they are made from "renewable resources" or "post-consumer materials" may contain corn products. Please call the ingredient manufacturer to verify the container's products.

Cornstarch

A powdered derivative of corn normally used as a thickener for fruit pies, custards, puddings, gravies, stews, and some cakes. For persons with a corn allergy, you may use one of the following:

Arrowroot Powder, Arrowroot Flour, or Arrowroot Starch
From a dried, ground tuber grown in the West Indies, Florida, or Fiji. Dissolve in a small amount of cold water before using. Use ⅔ tablespoon arrowroot for each 1 tablespoon cornstarch used in recipe.

Kudzu or Kudu Powder
From the root of the kudzu vine, it is from the Bean family. The root is pounded and mixed with water. The water is then drained from the starchy silt and the process repeated. Sift out lumps, then dissolve the sifted powder in a small amount of cold water before using. Use ⅓ to ½ tablespoon kudzu for each 1 tablespoon cornstarch used in recipe.

Potato Flour

From cooked, dried, and ground white potatoes. Potatoes are from the Potato family. Use 1 tablespoon potato flour for each 1 tablespoon cornstarch used in recipe.

Potato Starch

From raw white potatoes. Potatoes are ground and mixed with water. The starchy silt is then removed and dried. Dissolve in a small amount of cold water before using. Use 1 tablespoon potato starch for each 1 tablespoon cornstarch used in recipe.

Rice Flour

Made from the cooked, dried, and ground rice kernels. Dissolve in a small amount of cold water before using. If possible, purchase "Mochika" or "sweet" rice flour, which is a waxier type of rice and thickens better with fewer lumps. Use 1 tablespoon rice flour for each 1 tablespoon cornstarch used in recipe.

Tapioca

Made from the cooked, ground cassava root. It is from the Spurge family. Depending on the recipe, it may be helpful to dissolve the tapioca pearls in hot or cold water before using; see container for helpful hints. There are a variety of tapiocas available; small pearled quick-cooking tapioca was used in creating these recipes. Use 4 teaspoons tapioca for each 1 tablespoon cornstarch used in recipe.

Corn Syrup

Normally used as a sweetener for caramel desserts, as a clear sweetener and thickener for pies, or as the basis for glazes on tarts. Also known by trade and other names as caramel, cerelose, dextrose, fructose, glucose, Karo syrup, maltodextrin, and sucrose. Substitute 1 cup of granulated sugar melted over low heat with ¼ cup water for each 1 cup of corn syrup used in recipe.

Cow's Milk

Normally used to provide fats to assist baked goods in rising and to provide necessary liquids in batters. Commonly used names for cow's milk products and derivatives are casein, curd, lactalbumin, lactoglobulin, lactose, sodium caseinate, whey, and rennet. Note that calcium carbonate and calcium lactate are not dairy-derived ingredients. Also, any product with the word "Pareve" or "Parve" is guaranteed to be dairy free. There are a variety of alternatives to cow's milk products in the dairy section of health food grocery stores. We have used the following as substitutions in equivalent proportions to amounts used in recipes:

- almond milk
- coconut milk
- fruit juices, fruit concentrates, or fruit purees (you may want to slightly increase the fat content in the recipe, using margarine or oil, if you find the baked good does not rise well using a nonfat product)
- goat's milk*
- hemp milk
- oat milk
- powdered or dried-milk alternatives such as soy milk powder, Better Than Milk Rice *or* Meyenberg goat's milk powder,* reconstituted with water
- rice milk
- soy milk

*Note: Goat's milk products can sometimes be good substitutes for a person who is sensitive to cow's milk. However, various constituents of cow's milk may also be present in goat's milk because of the similar protein compositions. It would be helpful to determine what is causing the allergic reaction before switching to goat's milk products. Most of the information readily available about cow's milk concerns milk fat, lactose, casein, and whey. Neither milk fat nor lactose has been shown to cause allergic reactions. A person with an allergy to cow's milk is reacting to the casein, the whey, or both. The casein in cow's milk is similar to the casein in goat's milk. If the reaction can be narrowed down to the casein component, then goat's milk should not be used. The most allergic component in cow's milk is the Beta-lactoglobulin, which is the major milk protein found in whey. The whey in goat's milk seems to be different from the whey in cow's milk. If goat's milk can be tolerated and cow's milk causes a reaction, then the sensitivity is probably to the whey, and the casein can be tolerated. Casein is also found in most soy and almond cheeses; it is the ingredient that allows the cheese to melt and to resemble cow's milk cheese. If casein can be tolerated, then most alternative cheeses are allowable. If casein is the allergen, please avoid soy, rice, almond, and other cheeses that contain it.

Can a person with a cow's milk allergy tolerate the special cow's milks formulated with the lactose-digesting enzyme? Probably not. Lactose intolerance is often mistakenly confused with a milk allergy. These are two different things: in an allergic reaction, the symptoms are produced when an allergen causes histamines to be released in the body cells. This release brings on the allergic symptoms. In contrast, lactose intolerance is due to a lack of the lactose-digesting enzyme in the body. Symptoms of lactose intolerance can include stomachaches, gas, bloating, and diarrhea. Therefore, the person with a cow's milk allergy will not be able to tolerate the special cow's milks formulated with the lactose-digesting enzyme.

Egg and Egg Whites

Used to thicken puddings and custards; to help baked goods rise; to clear soups like consommés and bouillons; to make meringues, frostings, marshmallows, and marshmallow sauce; to make mayonnaise, hollandaise, and many salad dressings. Also called *albumin*. Substitute one of the following for one egg:

- 1 teaspoon Ener-G Egg Replacer powder (contains white potato starch) dissolved in 2 tablespoons cold water
- ½ teaspoon baking powder
- ¼ teaspoon baking powder dissolved in 1 tablespoon cold water
- 1 tablespoon vinegar
- 2 egg yolks, carefully separated from the whites
- 1 teaspoon baking powder mixed with 1 teaspoon vinegar
- 1 tablespoon ground flax seed
- ½ banana, mashed
- ¼ cup unsweetened applesauce

Margarine

Normally used to provide fats to assist baked goods in rising. Many margarines use whey or lactose, both of which are cow's milk products. Use a nondairy (and non-corn oil, if corn is an allergen) margarine *or* an allowable (non-corn) mild tasting oil. Any product with the word "Pareve" or "Parve" is guaranteed to be dairy free.

Oil

Normally used to provide fats to assist baked goods in rising and to provide necessary liquids in batters. Many vegetable oils may also contain some corn and/or peanut oil; use a pure type, such as flax, olive, coconut, *or* canola oil to be sure you are avoiding allergens. Another alternative is an all-vegetable shortening made from organic palm oil from Spectrum Naturals *or* Earth Balance's vegan all-natural shortening. A mild tasting oil or shortening will work best as a substitute for butter or margarine in the recipes.

Salt

Normally used as a seasoning in cooked foods and to assist the chemical reaction for helping baked goods rise. Most commercial iodized table salts contain dextrose (a corn product) as a stabilizing ingredient, and many of those also have sodium silicoaluminate, an aluminum by-product, which may concern you as it does us. Some manufacturers offer iodine-free table and cooking salts that do not contain dextrose. Many local grocery stores now carry sea salt and "pickling" or "preserving" salts, which work just as well as table salt for cooking or baking, and are dextrose free and sodium silicoaluminate free, and we find them a much tastier ingredient. If you are concerned about a lack of iodine in your child's diet and the resultant possible impact on their thyroid, other good sources of iodine include shellfish, saltwater fish, dried seaweed, cod liver oil, and vegetables grown very near an ocean. Note that kosher or "sour" salt is *not* an allowable substitute for table salt for baking or to replace table salt.

Substitute sea salt in equivalent amounts.

Vanilla

Normally used to provide flavoring for baked goods. From the vainilla ("little scabbard" in Spanish) orchid in the Orchid family. Most commercial vanilla extracts and vanilla flavorings have corn syrup added as a sweetener. Most also use grain (corn or wheat) alcohol as the base in the extraction process.

Substitute any of the following in equivalent portions used in a recipe:

- Acquavit (made from rice, yeast)
- Arak (made from oats, coconut, cane, yeast)
- Brandy (made from grapes)
- Cognac (made from brandy)
- Okolehao (made from rice, taro, cane)
- Rum, U.S. or Jamaican (made from grapes, cane, yeast)
- Sake (made from rice, yeast)
- Scotch, unblended single malt (does not contain corn, wheat, or potato)
- Vodka (usually made from potatoes; verify ingredients)
- Very strong cold black coffee

To make your own vanilla extract: Chop 1 pound vanilla beans and place them in a large container. Add ½ gallon of any allowable clear alcohol and let steep for at least four weeks. Strain out the chopped beans and store the vanilla extract in a tightly sealed jar. You can also slice 2 vanilla beans lengthwise, scrape out the tiny seeds, and add them to your mixture before cooking or baking. You can slice 1 vanilla bean lengthwise and add it to the sauce or custard as it is cooking; remember to remove the bean pod before serving. *Or* make vanilla sugar and use in equivalent amounts in recipes by placing 1 whole vanilla bean in a large covered jar with granulated sugar, tightly sealed. The vanilla flavor will intensify the longer you leave the bean in the sugar.

Vinegar

Normally used with other ingredients to assist baked goods in rising. White vinegars are distilled from a variety of grains, fruits, and vegetables, while cider (brown) vinegar normally uses apple cider as its base. Since cider vinegar usually has as high a level of acidity (the important factor in baking, cooking, and pickling) as white vinegar, people with grain and potato allergies may use cider vinegar with confidence. Another alternative for cooking but not as much for baking is balsamic vinegar, which is distilled from wine. It costs more than cider vinegar and has an extremely vigorous taste.

Xanthan Gum

Normally used in gluten-free recipes as a binding agent. Xanthan gum is created from corn syrup and sucrose. Guar gum is an acceptable substitute; use the equivalent amount called for in the recipes.

BAKING INGREDIENTS SUBSTITUTION CHARTS

The following chart gives alternatives for common allergens in baking ingredients. Use the equivalent amount for the substitute ingredient unless otherwise specified.

Please be sure that the substitutes you choose do not contain the allergens you are trying to avoid. This is particularly important with multiple allergies. For example, when avoiding cow's milk dairy and corn, be sure the carob chips you are using do not contain whey or corn syrup sweeteners.

ALTERNATIVE INGREDIENTS CHART

COMMON INGREDIENT	ALLERGEN-FREE SUBSTITUTION
1 teaspoon baking powder	•½ teaspoon cream of tartar and ½ teaspoon baking soda •1 teaspoon Featherweight *or* Hain *or* Whole Foods' 365 brand *or* other cereal-free baking powder
butter	•goat's milk butter •nondairy (whey and lactose free), non-corn oil margarine •mild tasting corn-free oil •soft tofu (not low fat), mashed or blended
chocolate	carob
confectioners' sugar	•homemade (see recipe, page 22) •Agave powder inulin, equivalent amounts as used in recipes
1 tablespoon cornstarch	•⅔ tablespoon arrowroot flour •⅓ to ½ tablespoon kudzu powder •1 tablespoon potato flour *or* potato starch •1 tablespoon rice flour •4 teaspoons tapioca flour
1 cup corn syrup	1 cup granulated sugar melted with ¼ cup water
cow's milk	•almond milk •coconut milk •fruit juices, concentrates, *or* purees •goat's milk •reconstituted nondairy powdered milk •rice milk •soy milk
1 egg	1½ teaspoons Ener-G Egg Replacer powder vigorously mixed with 2 tablespoons cold water ½ teaspoon baking powder ¼ teaspoon baking powder mixed with 1 tablespoon cold water 1 tablespoon vinegar 2 egg yolks, carefully separated from the whites
margarine	•coconut oil •mild tasting corn-free oil •nondairy (whey and lactose free), non-corn oil margarine
salt	sea salt
vanilla extract, alcohol-free	•acquavit •arak •brandy •coffee, very strong and cold •homemade (see recipe, pages 35–36) •okolehao •rum, U.S. or Jamaican •sake •scotch, unblended single malt •vanilla extract or flavor, alcohol-free •vodka
xanthan gum	guar gum

ITEMS AND ALLERGENS CHART

The following chart lists common ingredients and their corresponding allergens. Refer to pages 29–36 for a detailed description of each item and why it may be an allergen for your child.

ITEM	ALLERGEN					
	WHEAT	EGG	CORN	DAIRY	NUT	CHOCOLATE
FLOUR	X		X			
BAKING POWDER			X			
BUTTER				X		
CHOCOLATE		X	X	X		X
CONFECTIONERS' SUGAR			X			
CORNSTARCH			X			
CORN SYRUP			X			
COW'S MILK				X		
EGG		X				
MARGARINE			X	X		
OIL			X		X	
SALT			X			
VANILLA	X		X			
VINEGAR			X			
YEAST	X					
XANTHAN GUM			X			
XYLITOL			X			

STOCKING YOUR PANTRY

The following items are necessary in the allergen-free kitchen. Most of these items are readily available at supermarkets or health food stores. If you have difficulty finding any of these products at your local store, check chapters 11 and 13 for a listing of manufacturers and suppliers to buy from directly.

baking powder, cereal-free

baking soda

canned coconut milk

chocolate *or* carob chips

cocoa *or* carob powder

cow's milk alternatives for butter and milk

Ener-G Egg Replacer powder

flour alternatives

margarine, allowable

oil, noncorn, non-nut

potato starch

sea salt, no additives

tapioca, flour and small pearled

vanilla extract or flavoring, alcohol-free

vinegar, cider

THE WELL-EQUIPPED KITCHEN

The following list comprises most of the basic equipment needed, but not required, for the recipes in this book.

blender

bowls, assorted sizes for mixing batters and doughs, microwave-safe plastic and glass

bundt pan

cake pans, 8 inch round or square and 13 by 9-inches rectangular

casserole dishes, 1½ quart and 2½ quart, microwave safe, in any shape with covers

cookie sheets, preferably insulated

cooling racks

cupcake papers, regular and large

cupcake tins, one large 6-well tin and one regular 12-well tin

electric mixer

food processor

frying pan, large

grater

griddle

jars with lids, 8 ounce and 16 ounce

knife, blunt table

knife, sharp

ladle, large

loaf pan, 5 by 9-inches

measuring cups, from 1/8 cup to 1 cup

measuring spoons, from 1/8 teaspoon to 1 tablespoon

microwave oven

microwave-safe dish, 8 inches square

paring knife

pastry cutter

peeler

pie pan, 9 inches

pot, 2 gallon or larger, nonaluminum

pot, 2½ quart double boiler, nonaluminum, with cover

rolling pin

sandwich toothpicks (longer and larger than the round toothpicks, and easier to use when testing baked goods in the oven for doneness)

saucepans, small, medium, and large, nonaluminum, with covers

sifter

skillet, large

spatula, plastic or rubber

springform pan, 9 inches

spoons, large slotted, large mixing, and wooden

strainer

tart pan, 11 inches

waffle iron

Cakes, Cupcakes, and Frostings Without Fear

Having now lived through many years' worth of birthdays, countless parties, and school celebrations, we finally admit that cakes and cupcakes are a fact of life. Adapting our existing ingredients and our "stop at the bakery on the way home from work" lifestyle was a *major* change. We graduated from whole wheat and white flours to amaranth, barley, buckwheat, kamut, oat, potato, quinoa, rice, rye, soy, and spelt flours; we retraced our baking roots from cake mixes back to scratch; we tasted our way from 2 percent and skim milk to soy, rice, almond, and goat's milks; we mixed, kneaded, beat, and burned our way from simple recipes to line-by-line substitutions until we had desserts that were not just edible and pretty, but delicious too!

Light, airy cakes result from gases produced by leavening agents trapped inside flours, from air beaten into an egg or into a butter-and-sugar mixture, or from a combination of the two. Because our flours have different textures and gluten contents than the usual bleached, enriched flour made from wheat, and because we do not use whole eggs, butter, or sugar, we must make a special effort to create these trapped pockets of gases. The recipes call for mixing ingredients and beating batters by hand with a large spoon, preferably wooden; you may choose to use an electric mixer set on the lower settings. We have found, however, that using a food processor or a blender will make a batter that is too sticky and gluey and does not bake well. You may want to take a little extra time to cream the margarine or oil with the sweetener very thoroughly, as this will create a lot of little air pockets. You will also want to remember to have egg yolks and all liquids at room temperature. Adding cold ingredients forces out the air and allows the margarine or oil to harden. Sifting the Ener-G Egg Replacer powder, baking soda, or baking powder with the flours before adding them to the creamed mixture will insure an even distribution of leavening agents and create uniform air pockets as the cake bakes instead of producing only several large holes. Finally, while our recipes call for mixing flours into the batter completely, too much mixing will beat the air pockets out of the creamed ingredients.

We found that pan sizes were variable: if the recipe calls for a 13 by 9-inch pan but you only have two 8-inch pans, go ahead! You might find you like the cake better as a layer cake. All of the cake recipes call for an 8-inch cake pan that can either be square or round, or you can use a 9-inch pan and the cooking time is the same. We also found that, unlike many commercial mixes and recipes, almost all of our cake recipes easily convert to cupcakes. When noted in the recipe that the cake can also be a cupcake dessert, use one 12-cup tin lined with cupcake papers and fill each paper one-half to two-thirds full with the batter. Just be sure to watch the clock, peek into your oven several times, and start the toothpick test earlier than required for cakes, as cupcakes bake more quickly.

We also found that mixing a gluten flour, such as oat or barley, with a "finer" non-gluten flour, such as rice or soy, makes a lighter, silkier cake. Many of our recipes list a variety of choices for you; the ingredient listed first in each line is the one with which we had the best success, but the alternatives will also work. If there is only one ingredient listed in a particular line, we have not found (or do not need) an allowable alternative for it. Please feel free to try your own combinations, and remember that as you get used to the different ways the substitute flours interact, you will become a pro at achieving your desired results.

Each recipe suggests a specific baking time. However, due to different altitudes and a range of oven temperature calibrations, we recommend you use a toothpick to determine when the cake is done. A cake is fully baked when a toothpick inserted into the center of the cake comes out clean. Dough clinging to the toothpick means the batter is not quite baked. Wait until the recommended baking time has elapsed, and begin checking at one-minute intervals if your first toothpick is doughy. Cakes will also start to pull away from the sides of the baking pan when almost baked. This is a good "eyeball" measure of doneness.

When fruits or berries are called for, you may use fresh or frozen. Frozen berries and small pieces of fruits will thaw and cook in the batter. Also, please note that whenever spices are an ingredient, we are using dried, ground spices, not whole. If whole spices are required, they will be specifically noted as such in the recipe.

Finally, since alternative-flour cakes are more fragile than bleached, enriched wheat flour cakes, try to serve them from the baking pan whenever possible to lessen the chance of the cake breaking or crumbling. You might want to try using parchment paper, corn-free waxed paper, or oiled brown paper to line the bottom of your cake pan before baking, as this will help the cake turn out more easily.

See pages 10–13 for the Cake and Cupcake Flour Chart to help you with these recipes.

Banana Cake

⅓ cup maple syrup

½ teaspoon vanilla extract, alcohol-free

½ cup mashed banana (1 small *or* ½ large banana)

¼ cup water *or* allowable milk

2 to 3 tablespoons margarine, shortening, *or* mild tasting oil*

½ cup arrowroot flour

2 teaspoons cinnamon

2 teaspoons baking powder

1 cup oat flour

½ cup barley flour *or* potato flour

½ cup rice flour *or* soy flour

This recipe is excellent for cupcakes, too!

Makes one 5 by 9-inch loaf cake *or* 12 cupcakes

Preheat oven to 325°F. Grease and flour one 5 by 9-inch loaf pan. For cupcakes, line one 12 cup cupcake tin with cupcake papers.

Combine maple syrup, vanilla, mashed bananas, water *or* milk, and margarine *or* oil. Mix well with spoon by hand or with an electric mixer on low setting. Add arrowroot flour, cinnamon, and baking powder and mix well. Add oat flour with barley *or* potato flour. Add rice *or* soy flour and mix well. If the batter is extremely stiff, add another ¼ cup water *or* milk.

Spoon into loaf pan.

Bake for 70 minutes or until inserted toothpick comes out clean.

If making cupcakes, fill each paper to two-thirds full and bake approximately 45 minutes or until inserted toothpick comes out clean.

Serve warm, or cooled and frosted. Coconut cream frosting (see page 65) is fun.

* If you are trying to reduce the amount of fat in your diet, you can omit the margarine or oil and still achieve delicious results.

Christmas Light Fruitcake

Nobody likes fruitcake, right? Wrong! This one delights everyone.

Makes one 5 by 9-inch loaf cake

Preheat oven to 350°F. Line one 5 by 9-inch loaf pan with parchment paper.

In a large bowl, mash the coconut cream until it is soft. Add the flours, baking powder, and Ener-G Egg Replacer powder; mix well. Add the spices; mix well. Add the honey *or* equivalent sweetener; mix well. Add the dried fruits and nuts; mix well to cover all fruits and nuts with the batter. At this point the batter will be very stiff. Add the vanilla *or* brandy *or* cognac and the orange juice; mix well.

Scrape the batter into the lined loaf pan.

Bake for 45 minutes, or until an inserted toothpick comes out clean.

Cool, slice, and serve.

½ cup coconut cream (the thick white part at the top of the can)

1 cup oat flour

1 cup barley flour

2 teaspoons baking powder

2 teaspoons Ener-G Egg Replacer powder

¼ teaspoon cinnamon

¼ teaspoon nutmeg

¼ teaspoon allspice

⅔ cup honey *or* equivalent liquid sweetener

½ cup chopped pitted dates

½ cup dried cranberries

½ cup dried cherries

½ cup allowable nuts, such as pecan *or* walnut *or* pistachio, shelled

1 teaspoon vanilla extract (alcohol-free) *or* brandy *or* cognac

⅔ cup orange juice

Gluten-Free Honey Cake

2 cups Bob's Red Mill Gluten Free All Purpose Baking Flour

1 teaspoon guar gum

½ teaspoon baking soda

2 teaspoons baking powder

1 teaspoon cinnamon

⅓ cup honey

¼ cup granulated sugar

¾ cup water

⅓ cup coconut oil *or* any mild tasting oil

A dear friend's little daughter cannot have gluten so we bring this for a Rosh Hashanah treat. She is so grateful!

Makes one 5 by 9-inch loaf cake

Preheat oven to 350°F. Grease one 5 by 9-inch insulated baking loaf pan.

In a medium bowl, mix 2 cups Bob's Flour with guar gum, baking soda, baking powder, and cinnamon; set aside. In microwave-safe dish or in a small saucepan, mix honey, sugar, and water; heat slowly until small bubbles appear. Pour this mixture into the bowl of an electric mixer; add the coconut oil and beat until well mixed. Slowly add the flour mixture, beating for 2 minutes until well mixed. Pour batter into loaf pan.

Bake for 30 to 35 minutes, until inserted toothpick comes out clean and the top of the cake has begun to crack.

For best flavor, cool completely after baking, wrap well, and refrigerate before serving.

Holiday Cake

This cake can be made well ahead of time: it keeps for weeks, and it toasts up great!

Makes one 5 by 9-inch loaf cake

Preheat oven to 350°F. Use one 5 by 9-inch loaf pan, ungreased and unfloured.

Mix rye and spelt flours with the baking soda, baking powder, and cinnamon; set aside. In a microwave–safe dish or on the stovetop in a small saucepan, mix honey, sugar *or* equivalent sweetener, and water; heat slowly until small bubbles begin to appear. Remove from the microwave or the stovetop; in the dish or saucepan add the margarine *or* oil; beat until well mixed. Pour this into the flour mixture and beat until well mixed. Pour batter into loaf pan.

Bake for 40 minutes, or until inserted toothpick comes out clean and the top of the cake has begun to crack.

Variation: You may use small amounts of soy, barley, or millet flours in place of some of the rye and spelt flours, for a silkier cake. You may also wish to make this a spice cake by reducing the cinnamon to ½ teaspoon and adding ⅛ teaspoon each of ground ginger, allspice, and cloves.

1 cup rye flour

1 cup spelt flour

½ teaspoon baking soda

2 teaspoons baking powder

1 teaspoon cinnamon

⅓ cup honey

½ cup sugar *or* equivalent sweetener

¾ cup water

⅓ cup softened margarine *or* mild tasting oil

Zucchini Bread

4½ teaspoons
Ener-G Egg Replacer
powder mixed with
6 tablespoons water

1 cup mild
tasting oil

2 cups sugar
or equivalent
sweetener

3 teaspoons vanilla,
alcohol-free

1½ cups oat flour

1½ cups millet flour

1 teaspoon salt

1 teaspoon
baking soda

3 teaspoons
cinnamon

¼ teaspoon
baking powder

2 cups grated
zucchini *or* yellow
summer squash

2 cups carob *or*
chocolate chips
(optional but tasty!)

*This bread tastes great and makes the whole house smell fantastic.
Even people who really aren't fond of zucchini love this.*

Makes two 5 by 9-inch loaves

Preheat oven to 325°F. Grease and flour two 5 by 9-inch loaf pans.

In a large bowl, beat Ener-G Egg Replacer powder mixture, oil, sugar, and vanilla together.

In another bowl, sift together the flours, salt, baking soda, cinnamon, and baking powder, and then beat into the wet mixture, ½ cup at a time, mixing well after each addition.

Mix in the grated zucchini (and carob chips *or* chocolate chips, if using). Pour the batter into two greased and floured loaf pans. Baked for 60 to 90 minutes, or until the tops are golden brown and an inserted knife comes out clean.

Cool in the loaf pans. May slice and serve warm or cooled.

Microwave Blueberry Upside-Down Cake

A great way to enjoy blueberries in the heat of the summer without warming up your kitchen.

Makes one 8-inch cake

In a microwave-safe, 8-inch baking dish, heat 1 tablespoon margarine for 35 seconds on HIGH.

For the topping: In a large microwave-safe bowl, stir blueberries, arrowroot flour, lemon peel, and sugar *or* equivalent sweetener until well mixed. Spoon the berry mixture evenly onto the melted margarine in baking dish.

For the cake: Using the same bowl, mix the sugar *or* equivalent sweetener with the softened margarine until creamy. Add vanilla and Ener-G Egg Replacer powder; mix well. Add allowable milk; mix well. Add oat flour and baking powder; mix well. Spoon the batter evenly over blueberries, using the back of the spoon to pat down and level the dough surface.

Microwave, uncovered, for 8 minutes on MEDIUM, then for 3 to 5 minutes on HIGH until inserted toothpick comes out clean. If your microwave does not have a revolving plate, rotate several times during cooking.

Cool for 10 minutes, then lay a large plate over the crust's surface and turn the dish over, tapping several times to loosen berries. Spoon any berries left in cooking dish onto the cake.

1 tablespoon margarine (for baking dish)

FRUIT TOPPING
2 cups blueberries, rinsed

1 teaspoon arrowroot flour

1 teaspoon grated lemon peel

¼ teaspoon sugar *or* equivalent sweetener

CAKE
½ cup sugar *or* equivalent sweetener

4 tablespoons margarine, softened

1 teaspoon vanilla extract, alcohol-free

½ teaspoon Ener-G Egg Replacer powder

⅓ cup allowable milk

1 cup oat flour

½ teaspoon baking powder

Carrot Cake

4 egg yolks

½ cup mild tasting oil

5 tablespoons hot water

1½ cups grated carrots

1½ teaspoons baking powder

½ teaspoon baking soda

½ teaspoon salt

1 teaspoon each ground nutmeg, cinnamon, and cloves

6 teaspoons Ener-G Egg Replacer powder

1 cup sugar *or* equivalent sweetener

½ cup oat flour

½ cup barley flour

½ cup soy flour *or* potato flour

So you want to serve something delicious but don't want to give up that nagging urge to be health conscious? Carrot cake fills your needs, with or without cream cheese frosting.

Makes one bundt cake *or* two 8-inch cakes

Preheat oven to 350°F. Grease and flour one 10-inch bundt cake pan *or* two 8-inch cake pans.

Mix egg yolks, oil, and hot water well. Add grated carrots and mix well. Add baking powder, baking soda, salt, nutmeg, cinnamon, cloves, and Ener-G Egg Replacer powder; mix well. Add sugar *or* equivalent sweetener; mix well. Add oat flour, barley flour, and soy *or* potato flour; mix well for another 5 to 10 minutes. Pour into cake pan.

Bake for 60 to 70 minutes or until inserted toothpick comes out clean.

Cool and frost with cream cheese frosting (see page 65).

Chocolate Cake

This is a simple one-bowl cake. It doubles easily for a large 13 by 9-inch sheet cake.

Makes one 8-inch cake *or* 12 cupcakes

Preheat oven to 350°F. Using some extra carob *or* cocoa powder, dust one ungreased 8-inch cake pan. If making cupcakes, line one 12-cup cupcake tin with cupcake papers.

In a large bowl, mix baking soda and coffee; add vanilla and baking powder and mix well. The batter will foam at this point: do not worry! Add salt, sugar *or* equivalent sweetener, and cocoa *or* carob powder; mix well. Add margarine *or* oil; mix well. Add flours; mix well.

If your batter is really stiff and unworkable, add a little water by teaspoonfuls until you like the consistency, but it should be a fairly thick batter. Spoon into cake pan.

Bake for 35 minutes or until inserted toothpick comes out clean.

If you are making cupcakes, start doing a toothpick check at 25 minutes.

Cool completely before serving.

To serve, frost (see frostings, this chapter) *or* place a paper lace doily on top of the baked cake, dust with homemade powdered sugar, and remove the doily.

½ teaspoon baking soda

1 cup black coffee, cooled

2 teaspoons vanilla extract, alcohol-free

2 teaspoons baking powder

½ teaspoon salt

½ cup sugar *or* equivalent sweetener

6 heaping tablespoons carob powder *or* cocoa powder

6 tablespoons softened margarine *or* shortening *or* mild tasting oil

½ cup oat flour

¾ cup flour (any one *or* combination of barley, rice, soy, *or* millet; *or* see chart, pages 10–13)

Chocolate Sour Cream Cake

This recipe was made as cupcakes for a child's birthday party, and the adults ate them all up! For a special treat, 10 ounces of mini-chocolate or carob chips will make this cake extra rich.

Makes two 8-inch cakes *or* one 13 by 9-inch cake *or* 16 cupcakes

⅔ cup softened margarine, shortening, mild tasting oil, *or* substitute

2 cups nondairy sour cream *or* nondairy plain yogurt

1 teaspoon vanilla extract, alcohol-free

3 teaspoons Ener-G Egg Replacer powder mixed with 1 tablespoon cold water

1 teaspoon salt

1¾ cups sugar *or* equivalent sweetener

½ teaspoon baking soda

¾ cup carob powder *or* cocoa powder

1¾ cups flour (e.g., ½ cup barley, ¼ cup rice, and 1 cup oat; *or* see chart, pages 10–13)

10 ounces mini-chocolate chips *or* mini-carob chips (optional)

Preheat oven to 350°F. Grease and flour two 8-inch cake pans *or* one 13 by 9-inch cake pan. If making cupcakes, line one 12-cup cupcake tin with cupcake papers and one 12-cup tin with an additional 4 cupcake papers.

In a large bowl, beat margarine *or* oil, sour cream *or* yogurt, and vanilla. Add Ener-G Egg Replacer powder already mixed with cold water; beat well. Add salt, sugar *or* equivalent sweetener, and baking soda; mix well. Add cocoa *or* carob powder; mix well. Add flour; mix well. If you are using mini-chips, stir them in at this point. Pour into cake pan(s). If making cupcakes, fill each cup ⅔ full.

Bake for 40 to 45 minutes or until inserted toothpick comes out clean.

If you are making cupcakes, start doing a toothpick check at 30 minutes.

Cool, frost if desired, and serve.

Quick Carob Cake

One day during breakfast, I realized my five-year-old son had no cake to take with him to a birthday party that afternoon. It seemed so unfair for him to go to a party and not have cake to eat. This cake was mixed together and into the oven in 10 minutes! He loved it!

Makes one 13 by 9-inch sheet cake *or* 16 to 18 cupcakes

Preheat oven to 350°F. Grease and flour one 13 by 9-inch cake pan. If making cupcakes, line one 12-cup cupcake tin with cupcake papers, and one additional 12-cup cupcake tin with 4 to 6 additional cupcake papers.

Mix sugar *or* equivalent sweetener, flour, carob *or* cocoa powder, baking soda, baking powder, and vinegar. Add oil *or* margarine, vanilla, and water, mixing continually until smooth. Pour into cake pan. If making cupcakes, fill each cup ⅔ full.

Bake for 35 to 40 minutes or until inserted toothpick comes out clean.

If you are making cupcakes, begin toothpick check at 20 minutes.

Cool, frost if desired, and serve. See frostings, this chapter.

2 cups sugar *or* equivalent sweetener

3 cups flour (e.g., 1 cup oat, 1 cup barley, and 1 cup potato; *or* see chart, pages 10–13)

½ cup carob powder *or* cocoa powder

2 teaspoons baking soda

1 teaspoon baking powder

2 tablespoons cider vinegar

⅔ cup mild tasting oil, shortening, *or* margarine

2 teaspoons vanilla extract, alcohol-free

2 cups cold water

Fudgy Brownie Cake by Grammy

1½ cups flour (e.g., 1 cup oat *or* spelt and ½ cup barley *or* millet; *or* see chart, pages 10–13)

⅓ cup carob powder *or* cocoa powder

1 cup sugar *or* equivalent sweetener

½ teaspoon salt

1 teaspoon baking soda

8 tablespoons melted margarine *or* mild tasting oil

2 tablespoons cider vinegar

2 teaspoons vanilla extract, alcohol-free

2 cups water

This cake can easily be doubled and baked in a 13 by 9-inch lightly greased and floured cake pan.

Makes one 8-inch cake

Preheat oven to 350°F. Use one greased and floured 8-inch cake pan.

Sift together the flour, carob *or* cocoa powder, sugar *or* equivalent sweetener, salt, and baking soda directly into the cake pan. Add the margarine *or* oil, vinegar, vanilla, and water, and gently fold the ingredients only until the larger lumps are dissolved.

Bake for 30 minutes or until an inserted toothpick comes out clean.

Cool, frost if desired, and serve.

Mini Chocolate Chip Cake

This easy, sweet cake looks as good as it tastes!

Makes one 8-inch cake

Preheat oven to 375°F. Grease one 8-inch cake pan.

Combine margarine *or* oil, water *or* allowable milk, and vanilla and mix well. Add brown sugar *or* equivalent sweetener, baking powder, and Ener-G Egg Replacer powder; mix well. Add the flour ½ cup at a time, mixing well after each addition. Add mini chocolate *or* carob chips; mix well. Pour into cake pan.

Bake for 30 minutes or until inserted toothpick comes out clean.

Cool, frost if desired, and serve.

¼ cup softened margarine *or* mild tasting oil

⅓ cup water *or* allowable milk

1 teaspoon vanilla extract, alcohol-free

1 cup light *or* dark brown sugar, packed, *or* equivalent sweetener

3 teaspoons baking powder

1 teaspoon Ener-G Egg Replacer powder

1 cup oat flour

½ cup barley flour

½ cup rice flour *or* soy flour

10 ounces mini chocolate chips *or* mini carob chips

TOPPING

2 tablespoons margarine *or* shortening, *or* mild tasting oil

¼ cup chopped almonds *or* macadamia nuts, *or* nuts of your choice

⅔ cup light *or* dark brown sugar, packed, *or* equivalent sweetener

FRUIT

8 ounces fresh *or* thawed frozen pineapple, peeled, cored, and cut into chunks

1 banana, sliced

CAKE

1 cup sugar *or* ¾ cup honey

½ cup softened margarine, shortening, *or* mild tasting oil

1 teaspoon vanilla extract, alcohol-free

⅔ cup soy milk *or* rice milk *or* other allowable milk

2 egg yolks *or* 3 tablespoons Ener-G Egg Replacer powder

½ cup flour (e.g., any one *or* combination of oat *or* spelt; *or* see chart, pages 10–13)

¾ cup uncooked oats, any type

1 tablespoon baking powder

Pineapple Banana Upside-Down Cake

This tropical combination of pineapples and bananas always makes our mouths water!

Makes one 8-inch cake

Preheat oven to 350°F. Use one 8-inch ungreased cake pan.

For the topping: Place the margarine *or* butter *or* oil, the nuts, and the brown sugar *or* equivalent sweetener into the cake pan; place the pan in the heated oven and leave it until the brown sugar *or* equivalent sweetener has begun to liquefy (usually a few minutes). Remove pan from oven. Stir until all three ingredients are well mixed.

For the fruit: Arrange the pineapple chunks and banana slices evenly on top of the topping mixture; set pan aside.

For the cake: In a large bowl, beat sugar *or* honey, allowable shortening *or* margarine *or* oil, and vanilla until smooth. Add allowable milk and egg yolks *or* Ener-G Egg Replacer powder and beat until smooth. Slowly add flour, oats, and baking powder, beating well to keep the batter smooth. Pour slowly and evenly over the fruit mixture in the baking pan.

Bake 45 to 50 minutes or until inserted toothpick comes out clean. Slide a blunt knife around the inside edges of the baking pan until the cake is loosened from the sides of the pan. Cover the baking pan completely with a large plate and, using oven mitts, hold the plate on tightly and flip the cake upside down onto the plate. Scrape out any remaining topping from the pan and spread it onto the cake top.

Cool before serving.

*My Kid's **Allergic to Everything** Dessert Cookbook*

Simple To Make Vinegar Cake

This is my mother's old-fashioned recipe that is really delicious, and kids sure are surprised when they bite into "vinegar cake" and get a mouthful of sweetness!

Makes one 8-inch cake

Preheat oven to 350°F. Use one 8-inch cake pan, ungreased and unfloured.

In the cake pan, mix together the flour, sugar *or* equivalent sweetener, cocoa *or* carob powder, baking soda, and salt. Make three well-spaced holes in the dry mixture with your finger; pour margarine *or* oil into the first hole, pour vinegar into the second hole, and pour vanilla into the third hole. Pour the cold water over all the mixture; with a fork, stir just until smooth.

Bake for 25 to 35 minutes, or until an inserted toothpick comes out clean.

Variation: Immediately after removing the baked cake from the oven, sprinkle carob or chocolate chips evenly over the top of the cake, or cover the top of the baked cake with a single layer of the chocolate or carob bars. Turn off the oven and put the cake back in for another 2 to 3 minutes until the chocolate or carob layer is melted. Cool and serve.

1½ cups flour (e.g., 1 cup oat and ½ cup barley, rice, *or* spelt; *or* see chart, pages 10–13)

1 cup sugar *or* equivalent sweetener

3 tablespoons cocoa powder *or* carob powder

1 teaspoon baking soda

½ teaspoon salt

5 tablespoons melted margarine *or* mild tasting oil

1 tablespoon cider vinegar

1 teaspoon vanilla extract, alcohol-free

1 cup cold water

12 ounces carob chips *or* chocolate chips *or* 6 carob *or* chocolate candy bars (optional)

Sponge Cake

1 cup oat flour

½ cup barley flour *or* potato flour

½ cup millet flour

1 cup sugar *or* equivalent sweetener

3 teaspoons baking powder

1 teaspoon Ener-G Egg Replacer powder

¼ cup plus 1 tablespoon mild tasting oil *or* softened margarine

1 teaspoon grated lemon *or* orange peel (optional)

½ cup cold water

This is a favorite at family gatherings as it appeals to a wide variety of tastes.

Makes one 8-inch cake

Preheat oven to 375°F. Grease one 8-inch cake pan.

Mix oat, barley *or* potato flour, and millet flour well. Add sugar *or* equivalent sweetener, baking powder, and Ener-G Egg Replacer powder; mix well. Cream in oil *or* margarine and lemon *or* orange peel; mix well. Add water; mix well until smooth. This is a somewhat stiff batter, more like a dough. If you feel it is too heavy and doughy, add cold water *or* any other cold liquid by teaspoonfuls until you have a workable batter, but it should still be doughy rather than runny. Pat batter into cake pan.

Bake for 35 minutes or until inserted toothpick comes out clean.

Cool and serve. Nondairy whipped cream is delicious on this cake!

Yummy Cake

This favorite and easy recipe is a lifesaver. With only four weeks to create a birthday cake recipe for my son's fifth birthday without using egg or wheat, this cake was frantically adapted from a regular cake recipe that used a little potato flour along with white cake flour. I substituted barley and oat flours for the white cake flour, along with making other allergen-free changes. He declared it "Yummy!"

Makes one 8-inch cake

Preheat oven to 375°F. Grease one 8-inch cake pan.

Mix potato, barley, and oat flours well. Add sugar *or* equivalent sweetener, baking powder, and Ener-G Egg Replacer powder; mix well. Cream in oil *or* shortening *or* margarine; mix well. Add water *or* allowable milk and lemon extract *or* peel; mix well. At this point, the batter should be like smooth mashed potatoes, but not have a really stiff texture. If your batter seems a little too stiff or dry, add more liquid (water *or* allowable milk) by teaspoonfuls until you are happy with the batter's consistency. Pour into cake pan.

Bake for 30 minutes or until the middle is firm to your touch.

Cool, frost if desired, and serve. Lemon Magic Frosting is nice on this cake (page 66).

Variation: You can substitute orange extract, grated orange peel, or almond extract for the lemon extract or peel.

½ cup potato flour

½ cup barley flour

1 cup oat flour

1 cup sugar
or equivalent sweetener

3 teaspoons baking powder

1 teaspoon Ener-G Egg Replacer powder

⅔ cup mild tasting oil **or** shortening **or** softened margarine

⅓ cup water **or** allowable milk

1 teaspoon lemon extract, alcohol-free **or** grated lemon peel

Booger Cupcakes

½ cup unsweetened shredded coconut, soaked in ½ teaspoon green food coloring

1 cup spelt flour

1 cup barley *or* other mild flour

1 teaspoon Ener-G Egg Replacer powder

1 teaspoon baking powder

⅔ cup honey

4 tablespoons coconut cream (the thick white part at the top of the can), softened

1 teaspoon vanilla extract, alcohol-free

2 teaspoons lime juice

½ teaspoon green food coloring (for cupcake batter)

¼ cup water *or* limeade

Kids sure do come up with questions! "Why are boogers green, Mommy?" "So they can go in the special cupcakes, lovey."

Makes approximately 12 regular cupcakes

Preheat oven to 350°F. Line one 12-cup cupcake tin with cupcake papers.

In a small bowl, soak the shredded coconut in the green food coloring, mixing well to spread the color around.

In a large bowl, mix the spelt, the barley *or* other mild flour, Ener-G Egg Replacer powder, and baking powder. Add the honey, coconut cream, vanilla, lime juice, and green food coloring. Beat until all ingredients are well mixed. Add the water *or* limeade and beat in until all liquids are absorbed. If the batter seems a little stiff, add more water *or* limeade by teaspoonfuls until the batter is loose enough to drip off the spoon. Add the shredded coconut and mix well. Fill the cupcake papers ¾ full.

Bake for 22 minutes or until an inserted toothpick comes out clean.

The coconut cream frosting is nice on these! Add some green food coloring to maintain the gross-out factor.

Da ChocoBomb Cupcakes

We love these because they really satisfy that choco-carob craving.

Makes 12 cupcakes

Preheat oven to 350°F. Line one 12-cup cupcake tin with cupcake papers.

In a large bowl, mix the oat flour, spelt flour, cocoa *or* carob powder, baking powder, baking soda, salt, and Ener-G Egg Replacer powder until completely mixed. Stir in the margarine *or* allowable shortening *or* coconut cream, vanilla, agave nectar, and milk *or* yogurt.

Drop one tablespoon of batter into each cupcake paper and pat it down.

In a separate small bowl, mix the frozen mini chips and the margarine *or* allowable shortening *or* coconut cream until all the mini chips stick together. Drop a teaspoonful of the mini-chip mixture into the center of the batter in each cupcake paper.

Add another tablespoon of batter on top of the mini chip mixture until the cupcake papers are ¾ full.

Bake for 25 minutes or until an inserted toothpick comes out clear of batter. Start checking at 20 minutes.

Note: The toothpick will show a lot of the melted mini chips, but that is smoother and glossier than uncooked batter—you'll be able to tell. Trust me!

1 cup oat flour

1 cup spelt flour

½ cup cocoa *or* carob powder

1 teaspoon baking powder

1 teaspoon baking soda

¼ teaspoon salt

1½ teaspoon Ener-G Egg Replacer powder

½ cup margarine *or* allowable shortening *or* coconut cream (the thick white cream at the top of the can), softened

1 teaspoon vanilla extract, alcohol-free

¼ cup agave nectar, dark or light

½ cup any allowable milk (such as oat *or* coconut) *or* plain *or* vanilla allowable yogurt

½ cup mini chocolate *or* mini carob chips, frozen

½ tablespoon coconut cream *or* margarine *or* allowable shortening

Swirly Holiday Cupcakes

1 cup oat flour

1 cup barley flour

3 teaspoons Ener-G Egg Replacer powder

2 teaspoons baking powder

¼ teaspoon salt

½ cup honey

½ cup coconut milk *or* allowable milk

Organic food colorings, liquid or gel

These can be made for Hannukah or Christmas, just choose your colors.

Makes 12 cupcakes

Preheat oven to 350°F. Line one 12-cup cupcake tin with cupcake papers.

In a medium bowl, mix the oat flour, barley flour, Ener-G Egg Replacer powder, baking powder, and salt until completely blended. Stir in the honey and allowable milk; beat for 2 minutes or until no lumps are present.

Fill the cupcake papers ⅔ full. Drizzle several drops of food coloring on the top of each unbaked cupcake. With a sandwich toothpick, swirl the food coloring around.

Bake for 14 minutes or until an inserted toothpick comes out clean.

Variation: In a small bowl, mix 1 tablespoon of coconut cream with 3 tablespoons agave inulin powder and drizzle 1 teaspoonful on top of each unbaked cupcake. The mixture will bake into a translucent glaze.

Tropical Cupcakes

We like these because of the juicy burst of fruit flavors.

Makes 12 cupcakes

Preheat oven to 350°F. Line one 12-cup cupcake tin with cupcake papers.

In a small bowl, snip the dried fruit into small pieces (about the size of M&M candies). Add the dried cherries and the juice. Mix well and set aside.

In a large bowl, mix the spelt flour, amaranth flour, coconut cream, agave inulin powder, Ener-G Egg Replacer powder, baking soda, and salt until thoroughly blended. Add the dried fruit mixture and mix well. Add the juice and beat for 1 minute. If the batter still seems a little stiff, add more juice 1 tablespoon at a time until the batter is thick but not runny. Spoon into cupcake papers until ⅔ filled.

Bake for 16 minutes or until an inserted toothpick comes out clean. Cool completely before frosting. The Banana-Chocolate frosting is good with these (page 64)!

Note: Fresh fruits are too mushy for this recipe; dried fruits really do work best.

Variation: Substitute blueberry or pomegranate juice and the cupcakes will turn dark purple. My kids call them Brontosaurus Cupcakes!

DRIED FRUIT MIXTURE

6 pieces dried mango

3 dried papaya strips, 3 inches long

¼ cup dried cherries

2 dried apricots

1 tablespoon orange juice, lemonade, *or* limeade

BATTER

1 cup amaranth flour

1 cup spelt flour

4 tablespoons coconut cream (the thick white cream at the top of the can), softened

4 teaspoons agave inulin powder

1½ teaspoons Ener-G Egg Replacer powder

1 teaspoon baking soda

¼ teaspoon salt

¾ cup orange juice, lemonade, *or* limeade

Icings and Frostings

Banana-Chocolate Frosting

1 cup margarine *or* soft tofu

2 tablespoons carob powder *or* cocoa powder

1 large banana, peeled

1 tablespoon honey

Add some chocolate flavor to fruit cupcakes or fruit flavor to your chocolate cakes!

Will frost one 8-inch cake or 12 cupcakes, completely cooled

Place all ingredients in food processor or blender; puree until smooth.

Cherry Compote

2 pounds fresh tart *or* sweet cherries, rinsed and pitted

¼ cup granulated sugar *or* equivalent sweetener

1 teaspoon kirsch (cherry brandy liqueur)

2 to 3 teaspoons balsamic vinegar

This is a great topping for ice cream or cake!

Makes approximately 4 cups

Put the cherries in a large skillet and sprinkle them with the sugar *or* equivalent sweetener. Heat over high heat on top of the stove, shaking the pan often until the sweetener melts and the cherries begin to feel soft. Add kirsch and vinegar and gently shake the pan for another 30 seconds. Place the compote in a large bowl and refrigerate for at least one hour.

*My Kid's **Allergic to Everything** Dessert Cookbook*

Coconut Cream Frosting

This is so sweet and easy!

Will frost one 8-inch cake *or* 12 cupcakes, completely cooled

1 cup plain *or* vanilla agave inulin powder

1 tablespoon coconut cream (the thick white cream that collects at the top of the can)

2 tablespoons coconut milk (the liquid at the bottom of the can)

Place all ingredients in a small but deep bowl; using an electric mixer, start on low so as not to blow the powder out of the bowl and mix until lumpy. Increase the speeds on the mixer until at the highest speed; continue mixing for at least 2 minutes.

Drizzle over the cake or cupcakes to frost, as this is extremely sweet!

Variation: Scrape the frosting into a microwave-safe bowl and heat for 1 minute; this will turn the frosting into a clearer, dark, honey-like frosting with a caramel flavor.

Cream Cheese Frosting

The perfect frosting for the traditional carrot cake that we remember from childhood.

Will frost one 8-inch cake *or* 12 cupcakes, completely cooled

8 ounces nondairy cream cheese, softened

½ cup or more confectioners' sugar, to taste

1 teaspoon vanilla extract, alcohol-free

In a medium bowl, beat confectioners' sugar and vanilla into the cream cheese. To make your own confectioners' sugar, see page 22. If it's not sweet enough, add more confectioners' sugar, 1 tablespoon at a time.

Magic Frosting

¼ cup margarine *or* shortening

¼ cup honey *or* maple syrup

2 to 3 tablespoons rice milk *or* soy milk *or* fruit juice*

1 teaspoon any alcohol-free flavoring extract: vanilla, lemon, mint, rum, etc.

⅔ cup Better Than Milk powder *or* goat's milk powder *or* soy milk powder, unreconstituted

Fruit juice of your choice for color (optional)

Carob powder *or* cocoa powder (Optional)

*Note: You may substitute a fruit juice in place of the milk; however, a very acidic juice like orange or pineapple will not work well. Try using apple juice, pear juice, or peach nectar.

This frosting can be made in many colors and flavors.

Will frost one 8-inch cake *or* 12 cupcakes, completely cooled

Cream together margarine *or* shortening and honey *or* maple syrup. Mix in milk *or* juice and your chosen flavoring extract. Add your selected milk powder, and continue beating until the frosting is light and fluffy. At this point, if the frosting is too stiff, add more milk, little by little, to achieve the desired consistency.

Variation: Color may be created by adding a little cranberry juice for a pink frosting or a little purple grape juice for a lavender frosting. A chocolate flavor may be achieved by creaming in 1/4 cup carob powder or cocoa powder immediately after adding the milk. Taste to test for desired sweetness. This would not work well, however, if you are using a fruit juice in place of the milk.

Whipped Topping

This is luscious on strawberry shortcake.

Put milk, sugar *or* equivalent sweetener, and vanilla in a blender. Blend on low for 30 seconds, then on high for 30 seconds. Remove the lid plug and pour in the guar gum. Blend for another 15 to 20 seconds or until the mixture forms a mound. Serve immediately.

1 cup chilled allowable milk

1½ tablespoons sugar *or* equivalent sweetener

1 teaspoon vanilla extract, alcohol-free

1 teaspoon guar gum

Other Toppings Ideas

Sliced fresh seasonal organic fruits or berries will always dress up the plainest cakes.

Jams and jellies (corn-syrup free) can be spread between cooled cake layers or drizzled on the top of a still-hot cake to make a fancy dessert. See Breakfast Ideas (chapter 10) to create your own homemade jams and jellies.

Chocolate chips or carob chips may be melted in the microwave or on top of the stove in a small saucepan and quickly drizzled over the top of your cake, cupcakes, or over cut fruit.

Chocolate candy bars or chocolate chips or carob chips may be placed on top of a completely baked cake, which is then returned to the oven, now turned off, for several minutes to allow the chocolate or carob to melt.

A nondairy whipped topping is delightful for cooled cakes or cupcakes.

The Almost-Chocolate Pudding (page 130) is great on completely cooled cakes and cupcakes.

Crusts and Toppings

Some pastry chefs talk about kneading pie crusts until the fat (butter, margarine, oil, or shortening) is well mixed into the flour. Some warn of dire consequences if the dough is kneaded or rolled even a moment longer than necessary. Some require ice water for a flaky crust, some use vinegar, some swear by lard, and some will use only the best butter.

What works for you? Frankly, a crust, unless it is a pastry designed to be an integral part of the dessert, is only a thing to hold the fruit filling together until and as you eat it. Nice, easy to make, stable crust recipes for your favorite fillings follow.

A helpful note: We found an easy way to roll out a crust using plastic wrap. Take a sheet of plastic wrap a little larger than twice the size of the top of the pie pan; place the dough ball in the center of one-half of the plastic wrap; fold the other half over the dough ball, also centering that half-sheet. Using a rolling pin, begin to roll out a circle of dough, periodically lifting and repositioning the plastic wrap to avoid "wrinkles" in your crust, every now and then flipping the whole thing over and rolling out the other side. When the dough has reached the desired thickness and circumference, simply peel back the top layer of plastic wrap, slide your hand under the bottom layer, turn the crust over into your pie pan, using the plastic wrap to help you lift and tuck the dough completely into the pan and down its sides, then peel the plastic wrap off the top of the dough and throw it away! No floury mess, no sticky dough on your rolling pin, no counter to clean up!

The Pie Crust and Topping Flour Chart on pages 14–15 will help you select the flour or flour combinations that we have found work best for dough crusts and toppings.

Crusts

Coconut Crust

1 cup unsweetened shredded coconut

2 tablespoons mild tasting oil (safflower, coconut, etc.)

2 tablespoons honey

This pat-in-the-pan pastry is made with unsweetened shredded coconut. If you are a coconut lover, you will find many uses for this versatile crust.

Makes 1 crust

Combine all ingredients. Press into one 8-inch or 9-inch pie pan. Bake at 325°F for 5 to 8 minutes. Cool and fill with desired filling, then bake as directed.

Dough Crust

1 cup oat flour

½ cup barley flour

½ teaspoon salt

4 tablespoons allowable margarine *or* shortening

1 tablespoon mild tasting oil (safflower, canola, etc.)

4 tablespoons ice water

For traditional pie crust, you will turn to this Dough Crust time and time again. It is one of our favorites.

Makes 1 thick bottom crust *or* 1 normal bottom crust and 1 very thin top crust

Sift together the flours and the salt. Knead or cut in the margarine *or* shortening, then the oil, and gently knead in the water. Roll into a ball and flatten with your hands. Using a floured rolling pin, roll the dough out slowly until it is large enough to cover the bottom and sides of one 9-inch pie pan. Gently press the dough into the pie pan and bake at 325°F for 5 to 8 minutes, until the edges begin to turn golden, *or* fill with filling and bake as directed.

Note that this recipe will give you enough dough to also make a thin top crust, if you roll out a thinner ¼-inch bottom crust. You can roll out a very thin top crust, *or* use the dough for a lattice-top crust.

For a sweeter crust, add 1 tablespoon confectioners' sugar to the sifted flour and salt mixture, then proceed as above.

Sometimes bakers use lard for a very flaky crust. If you don't mind using an animal fat, lard is an allowable substitute for margarine or shortening.

*My Kid's **Allergic to Everything** Dessert Cookbook*

Granola Crust

This simple pie crust uses just three easy ingredients. It makes a great crust for fruit pies.

Makes 1 crust

Combine all ingredients. Press into one 8-inch or 9-inch pie pan. Bake at 325°F for 5 to 8 minutes. Cool and fill with desired filling, then bake as directed.

½ cup granola (see page 141)

2 tablespoons mild tasting oil (olive, canola, etc.)

2 tablespoons honey

Streusel Topping

We love this crispy topping on muffins, pies, cakes . . . or just about any dessert!

Makes topping for 1 pie *or* 1 cake

Place brown sugar *or* date sugar, cane sugar, and cinnamon in a bowl. Mix well. Add flour and mix well. Add allowable shortening *or* margarine and vanilla, mixing until the topping is coarse and crumbly. Add nuts, if using, and mix in well.

This topping may be used instead of a top dough crust on a pie. It also works well when used on cakes; just sprinkle the topping on the batter before baking.

⅓ cup light *or* dark brown sugar *or* date sugar, packed

2 tablespoons cane sugar

1½ teaspoon cinnamon

½ cup more glutinous flour (see chart, page 7)

¼ cup softened allowable shortening *or* softened allowable margarine

½ teaspoon vanilla extract, alcohol-free

1 cup chopped walnuts *or* pecans (optional)

Berry and Fruit Delights

Today's economy has made us stop and look at each other across the breakfast plates, the dinner dishes, the receipts at the checkout counter. Maybe our ancestors had a good idea—the more you make at home, the more you save! One area where you don't have to skimp is desserts, both retro and haute cuisine.

The variety of fruit and berry desserts across our country is amazing. Some of our favorite regional recipes were carried across the ocean by colonists and immigrants, then modified to suit the fruits and berries available in the new world.

Ever wonder which fruit to purchase and what information is hidden in the tiny labels in the produce bins at your supermarket? In addition to providing price and inventory information, these labels can also tell you where the produce came from. The four- and five-digit numbers on the stickers of bulk produce items are known as PLU (price look-up) codes. In addition to identification, price, and inventor, these stickers also designate if the produce was grown conventionally, organically, or with genetic modification. To figure out what you are buying, this is how to interpret the codes on the stickers: Items with four-digit PLU codes that begin with the number 3 or 4 are conventionally grown (4011 for a conventionally grown banana). Organically grown produce has five digit codes beginning with the number 9 (94011 for organic yellow bananas), but an 8 prefix indicates genetically modified food (84011 for genetically modified bananas).

To peel or not to peel, that is the question. We feel it's a personal choice. Nutrients and fiber are lost when the peel is discarded; however, purists feel that peel does not bake well. Do whatever you prefer. If you want to peel soft-skinned fruit, dip them into boiling water for 30 seconds, then remove with a slotted spoon and plunge them into ice water. Slip off the peels.

Some fruits adapt well to any recipe, while some are too dry or too juicy to substitute easily. Pears, for example, may differ greatly in variety, but are very similar in cooking and baking qualities. Apple varieties, however, differ greatly. Red Delicious and Gala

BUCKLE
Related to coffeecake. Fresh fruit is folded into a flour-and-butter batter, covered with a crunchy topping, and baked into a cakelike dessert.

CLAFOUTI
Fruit is stirred into a custard mixture and baked in a pie crust shell.

COBBLER
Sweetened fruit in thickened juice is covered with a biscuitlike crust and baked in a deep pan.

CRISP
Sweetened, thickened fruit is covered with a crunchy topping and baked in a deep pie pan or casserole dish.

CRUMBLE
Flour and margarine or shortening are cut together into a crumbly mixture, sprinkled on top of fruit, and baked in a pie pan.

apples do not cook well in pies; most remaining varieties such as Paula Red, Empire, McIntosh, Golden Delicious, IdaRed, Jonathan, Granny Smith, and Jonagold will bake nicely. Rome Beauty and Northern Spy are a little too tart to eat fresh, but cook up well. According to the Michigan Apple Committee, three medium-sized fresh apples weigh approximately 1 pound and six to eight medium-sized fresh apples will yield one nine-inch pie. Fresh blueberries may be stored in the refrigerator for up to 14 days if covered. To freeze berries, sort and rinse them and allow them to dry, then freeze them in a single layer on a cookie sheet. Once individually quick frozen, they may be transferred to air-tight containers and stored in the freezer for up to two years. Either fresh or frozen fruits and berries may be used in any of these recipes. An important tip—whenever berries are used in a dough or batter, coat them first in a separate bowl with a little bit of the flour from the recipe. This will keep them from sinking into the dough or batter when baking.

Most of all, have fun! Try different seasonal fresh fruits and berries. Splurge on a package of frozen berries in wintertime. Throw in a spice you haven't tried before, like fresh grated ginger with peaches or ground cloves with pears. Remember, even if the appearance is a bit unusual, it will still taste great.

Because certain flours work best for crusts and toppings, you will find all these recipes in the previous chapter. Most of the toppings are included with each recipe, but you can use a different one or create one of your own with a little guidance from chapter 5. You can also find a chart that describes some flours and their proportions that work well for the biscuit or dough toppings on pages 16–17 in chapter 1.

Nectarine or Peach Buckle

This cakelike dessert is rich and filled with fruit goodness. For a treat, try it with a scoop of dairy-free vanilla ice cream.

Makes 4 to 6 servings

Preheat oven to 375°F. Grease and flour one 1½-quart casserole dish.

For the batter: In a large bowl, beat sugar *or* equivalent sweetener, egg yolk, ginger, and margarine *or* shortening. Add milk and mix well for a smooth batter. Add 2 cups flour, baking powder, and salt, and mix well. Toss the nectarines *or* peaches in the remaining 1 tablespoon flour to keep them from sinking to the bottom of the batter. Slowly fold the floured fruit into the batter and pour into casserole dish.

For the topping: Mix sugar, flour, and cinnamon well in a small bowl. Using table knives or a pastry cutter, cut the margarine *or* shortening into the mixture until you have pea-sized crumbs. Sprinkle the topping onto the fruit batter.

Bake for 45 to 50 minutes, or until a toothpick inserted into the topping comes out clean. Serve warm or cooled.

BATTER FILLING

¾ cup sugar *or* equivalent sweetener

1 egg yolk

½ teaspoon freshly grated ginger (optional)

¼ cup softened margarine *or* shortening

½ cup allowable milk

2 cups plus 1 tablespoon flour (e.g., any one *or* combination of oat, amaranth, *or* spelt; *or* see chart, pages 16–17), divided

2 teaspoons baking powder

1 teaspoon salt

5–6 nectarines *or* peaches, pitted and sliced thin

TOPPING

½ cup sugar *or* equivalent granulated sweetener (such as coconut sap sugar)

⅓ cup any flour (such as oat, spelt, *or* amaranth *or* see chart, pages 16–17)

1 teaspoon cinnamon

¼ cup softened margarine *or* shortening

Blueberry Buckle

BATTER FILLING
¾ cup sugar
or equivalent
sweetener

1 egg yolk

¼ cup softened
margarine *or*
shortening

½ cup allowable
milk

2 cups, plus 1
tablespoon, flour,
reserved (any one
or combination of
oat *or* spelt; *or* see
chart, pages 16–17)

2 teaspoons baking
powder

1 teaspoon salt

2 cups fresh *or*
frozen blueberries

TOPPING
½ cup sugar
or granulated
sweetener (such as
coconut sap sugar)

⅓ cup flour (any one
or combination of
oat *or* spelt; *or* see
chart, pages 16–17)

1 teaspoon
cinnamon

¼ cup softened
margarine *or*
shortening

I make this at least three times when blueberries are in season. It's a great coffeecake, too.

Makes 4 to 6 servings

Preheat oven to 375°F. Grease and flour one 1½-quart casserole dish.

For the batter: In a large bowl, combine sugar *or* equivalent sweetener, egg yolk, and margarine *or* shortening. Add milk and mix well for a smooth batter. Add 2 cups flour, baking powder, and salt, and mix well. Toss blueberries in remaining 1 tablespoon flour to keep them from sinking to the bottom of the batter. Slowly fold floured blueberries into batter and pour into casserole dish.

For the topping: Mix sugar *or* granulated sweetener, flour, and cinnamon well in a small bowl. Using table knives or a pastry cutter, cut the margarine *or* shortening into the mixture until you have pea-sized crumbs. Sprinkle this mixture on top of the blueberry batter.

Bake for 45 to 50 minutes, or until a toothpick inserted into the topping comes out clean. Serve warm or cooled.

Variation: Blackberries may be substituted for the blueberries.

Apple Clafouti

This is one of those recipes that everyone asks for. It is easy enough to make for every day as well as for parties.

Makes 4 to 6 servings

Preheat oven to 350°F. Use 1 tablespoon of the margarine *or* shortening to grease one 1½-quart casserole dish.

Melt the remaining 7 tablespoons of margarine *or* shortening in a large skillet. Add apples and cook slowly, stirring occasionally, until apples have become browned, approximately 10 to 12 minutes. Add ⅓ cup of the sugar *or* equivalent sweetener, rum *or* brandy *or* cognac, and cinnamon. Mix well for 1 minute, then remove from heat and let stand for 15 minutes.

In a blender, combine milk, Ener-G Egg Replacer powder, and vanilla, and blend well. Add flour, salt, and remaining ⅓ cup of sugar *or* equivalent sweetener and blend well. Pour apple mixture into casserole dish.

Pour batter over apples.

Bake 45 minutes, or until batter has puffed up and turned golden. Serve warm.

8 tablespoons margarine *or* shortening, divided

3 large apples, peeled, cored, and thickly sliced

⅔ cup sugar *or* equivalent sweetener, divided

¼ cup dark rum *or* brandy *or* cognac

½ teaspoon cinnamon

1 cup allowable milk

4½ tablespoons Ener-G Egg Replacer powder

1 tablespoon vanilla extract, alcohol-free

½ cup oat flour

Pinch of salt

Quick Cherry Clafouti

¼ cup allowable milk

⅔ cup sugar *or* granulated sweetener (such as coconut sap sugar), divided

4½ tablespoons Ener-G Egg Replacer powder

1 tablespoon vanilla extract, alcohol-free

⅛ teaspoon salt

⅔ cup flour (e.g., any one *or* combination of oat *or* spelt; *or* see chart, pages 16–17)

3 cups fresh *or* thawed sweet *or* tart cherries, rinsed and pitted

This clafouti recipe is taken from an old country dessert recipe and has a batter that holds the cherries together beautifully. It's a tasty way to get the health and antioxidant benefits found in cherries.

Makes 4 to 6 servings

Preheat oven to 350° F. Grease one 1½-quart casserole dish.

In a blender, put milk, ⅓ cup of the sugar *or* equivalent sweetener, Ener-G Egg Replacer powder, vanilla, salt, and flour; blend at high speed for 1 minute. Pour some of the batter into the casserole dish until it is ¼ inch deep; bake 1 to 2 minutes, or until batter has slightly set. Spread the cherries over the baked batter and sprinkle with the remaining ⅓ cup sugar *or* equivalent sweetener. Pour remaining batter over the cherries, smoothing batter with the back of a spoon if necessary.

Bake for 60 minutes, or until an inserted toothpick comes out clean. Serve warm or cold.

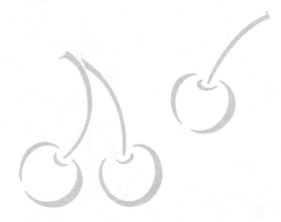

*My Kid's **Allergic to Everything** Dessert Cookbook*

Blueberry Cobbler

To make this sweet cobbler, blueberries are lightly sugared and flavored with lemon and cloves, and then topped with clouds of batter. Works best with fresh blueberries and is the perfect summer treat.

Makes 4 to 6 servings

Preheat oven to 400°F. Grease one 1½-quart casserole dish.

For the filling: In the casserole dish, mix berries, sugar *or* equivalent sweetener, arrowroot flour *or* potato starch, melted margarine *or* shortening, lemon juice, lemon peel, and cloves, and set aside.

For the batter: In a separate medium bowl, mix sugar *or* equivalent sweetener, flour, baking powder, and salt. Stir in egg yolk *or* Ener-G Egg Replacer powder, milk, and margarine *or* shortening, until a soft dough forms. If the dough seems too stiff, add another tablespoon of milk. Drop by spoonfuls on top of the blueberry mixture.

Bake 30 to 35 minutes or until filling begins to bubble and crust is golden brown. Serve warm or cool.

FILLING
2 pints blueberries, washed

¼ cup sugar *or* equivalent sweetener

2 tablespoons arrowroot flour *or* potato starch

1 tablespoon melted margarine *or* melted shortening

1 tablespoon lemon juice

1 teaspoon grated lemon peel

⅛ teaspoon ground clove

BATTER
¼ cup sugar *or* equivalent sweetener

¾ cup flour (e.g., any one *or* combination of oat *or* spelt; *or* see chart, pages 16–17)

¾ teaspoon baking powder

¼ teaspoon salt

1 egg yolk *or* 3 teaspoons Ener-G Egg Replacer powder

2 tablespoons allowable milk

2 tablespoons melted margarine *or* melted shortening

Cranberry-Pear Cobbler

FILLING

1 tablespoon margarine *or* shortening

5 medium pears, peeled, cored, and cut into ½-inch pieces

1 cup fresh *or* frozen cranberries

⅓ cup light *or* dark brown sugar, packed

⅓ cup sugar *or* equivalent sweetener

3 tablespoons arrowroot flour

2 tablespoons lemon juice

2 teaspoons cinnamon

½ teaspoon freshly grated ginger

TOPPING

1 cup flour (e.g., ½ cup oat and ½ cup barley; *or* see chart, pages 16–17)

¼ cup sugar *or* granulated sweetener (such as coconut sap sugar)

1 teaspoon baking powder

½ tablespoon Ener-G Egg Replacer powder

2 tablespoons cold allowable milk *or* ice water

¼ cup melted margarine *or* melted shortening, *or* mild tasting oil

The sweetness of the pears and tanginess of the cranberries make a sensational combination.

Makes 4 to 6 servings

Preheat oven to 325°F. Use one ungreased 1½-quart casserole dish.

For the filling: In a large frying pan, melt margarine *or* shortening. Add pears and cook over low flame until soft. Remove pan from heat and stir in cranberries, brown sugar, sugar *or* equivalent sweetener, arrowroot flour, lemon juice, cinnamon, and ginger. Mix well. Pour into casserole dish and set aside.

For the topping: In a separate medium bowl mix flour, sugar *or* granulated sweetener, baking powder, and Ener-G Egg Replacer powder. Add milk *or* ice water and stir only until combined. Fold in melted margarine *or* shortening *or* oil. Spoon topping evenly over filling. Bake 55 to 60 minutes, or until topping is browned and filling is bubbly. Serve warm or cold.

Microwave Berry Cobbler

Fresh, sweet, ripe summer berries make this an irresistible dessert. My family loves strawberries mixed with blueberries.

Makes 6 servings

For the filling: In a 1½-quart ungreased microwave-safe casserole dish, combine fruit, sugar *or* equivalent sweetener, arrowroot flour *or* potato starch, lemon juice, and lemon peel; microwave on high for 6 to 7 minutes or until it begins to bubble and thicken. Rotate and stir halfway through cooking. Let filling cool in the casserole dish for 20 to 30 minutes to allow it to finish thickening.

For the batter: In a separate medium bowl, mix flour, 1 tablespoon sugar *or* equivalent sweetener, baking soda, and nutmeg. Add yogurt and margarine *or* oil, and stir just until mixed. Divide dough into 6 equal balls, pat balls into half-inch thick biscuits, put in a separate 1½-quart microwave-safe dish, and set aside.

For the topping: In a separate small bowl, mix 1 tablespoon sugar *or* granulated sweetener and cinnamon; sprinkle evenly over the biscuits.

Microwave the biscuits on high for 2 to 3 minutes or until centers spring back when gently touched.

To serve, rewarm the filling and ladle over the biscuits.

*Note that if you are using peaches, try adding 1 teaspoon grated fresh ginger to really snap up that peach taste. Also, microwave the filling for an additional 4 to 5 minutes, as peaches are juicier and will take longer to cook and thicken.

FILLING

4 cups berries (all one kind, *or* mixed, *or* try 1 cup diced peaches with 3 cups berries*)

4 tablespoons sugar *or* equivalent sweetener

2 tablespoons arrowroot flour *or* potato starch

1 teaspoon lemon juice

½ teaspoon grated lemon peel

BATTER

½ cup flour (e.g., any one *or* combination of oat *or* spelt; *or* see chart, pages 16–17)

1 tablespoon sugar *or* equivalent sweetener

¼ teaspoon baking soda

⅛ teaspoon nutmeg

2 tablespoons nondairy yogurt

2 tablespoons melted margarine *or* mild tasting oil

TOPPING

1 tablespoon sugar *or* granulated sweetener (such as coconut sap sugar)

⅛ teaspoon cinnamon

Peach Cobbler

FILLING

8 large peaches, pitted and sliced

3 tablespoons sugar *or* granulated sweetener (such as coconut sap sugar)

3 tablespoons rum *or* cognac

2 tablespoons margarine *or* shortening

BATTER

½ cup flour (e.g., any one *or* combination of oat *or* spelt; *or* see chart, pages 16–17)

2½ teaspoons baking powder

½ teaspoon salt

8 tablespoons softened margarine *or* shortening

⅓ cup allowable milk

5 tablespoons sugar *or* granulated sweetener (such as coconut sap sugar)

Chef, restaurateur, and crazy dude Guy Fieri made his version of this traditional treat on **Guy's Big Bite.** *He prefers to use frozen sliced peaches to achieve a creamier filling. Remember: freezing breaks down the fruits and berries!*

Makes 6 to 8 servings

Preheat oven to 425°F. Grease one 2½-quart casserole dish.

For the filling: Place sliced peaches in casserole dish. Sprinkle with sugar *or* granulated sweetener and the rum; dot with margarine *or* shortening cut into small chunks.

For the batter: In a separate small bowl mix flour, baking powder, and salt. Using table knives or a pastry cutter, cut the margarine *or* shortening into the flour until the mixture is coarse and crumbly. Add milk and mix well until batter is very soft but not runny. If the batter still looks and feels stiff, add extra milk by teaspoonfuls until the batter consistency is very soft but not runny. Drop the batter in clumps over the peaches and refrigerate for 30 minutes. Remove from refrigerator, sprinkle 5 tablespoons sugar *or* granulated sweetener over the batter.

Bake for 30 minutes, or until the batter is puffy and golden. Serve warm.

My Kid's **Allergic to Everything** *Dessert Cookbook*

Apple Crisp

Serve this warm for a great winter dessert!

Makes one 9-inch crisp

Heat oven to 375°F. Use one ungreased 9-inch pie pan.

For the filling: Combine apples, pecans if using, and raisins in a large bowl. Place half of this mixture in the pie pan. Sprinkle ⅓ cup brown sugar over the fruit in the pie pan and top with the remaining half of the mixture.

For the topping: In a separate medium bowl, combine ⅓ cup brown sugar *or* equivalent sweetener, flour, oats, cinnamon, and nutmeg, mixing well. Using two table knives or a pastry cutter, cut in the margarine *or* shortening until the mixture is coarse and crumbly. Sprinkle this topping over the fruit mixture.

Bake for 30 to 35 minutes or until the apples are tender when a fork or toothpick is inserted.

FILLING

6 cups tart apples, cored, peeled, and sliced thin

¼ cup chopped pecans (optional)

¼ cup raisins

⅓ cup light *or* dark brown sugar, packed

TOPPING

⅓ cup light *or* dark brown sugar *or* equivalent sweetener, packed

⅓ cup flour (e.g., oat *or* spelt; *or* see chart, pages 16–17)

⅓ cup quick oats

½ teaspoon cinnamon

¼ teaspoon nutmeg

3 tablespoons margarine *or* shortening

Apricot Ginger Crisp

FILLING

⅓ cup light brown sugar *or* equivalent sweetener, packed

3 tablespoons flour (e.g., oat *or* spelt; *or* see chart, pages 16–17)

¼ cup peeled and freshly grated ginger

1 teaspoon cinnamon

Grated peel of 1 lemon

2½ pounds fresh apricots, pitted and halved (approximately 5 cups)

TOPPING

¾ cup flour (e.g., oat *or* spelt; *or* see chart, pages 16–17)

⅔ cup dark brown sugar, packed *or* equivalent sweetener

¼ teaspoon salt

¼ teaspoon cinnamon

½ teaspoon ground ginger powder

6 tablespoons cold margarine

When I bring this to family dinners, it disappears faster than the time I took to make it. Try baking it ahead of time for 20 minutes and then warming it up in the oven just before serving.

Makes one 9-inch crisp

Preheat oven to 375°F. Use one ungreased 1½-quart casserole dish.

For the filling: In a medium bowl, mix light brown sugar *or* equivalent sweetener, flour, fresh ginger, cinnamon, and lemon peel. Add apricots; thoroughly toss to coat fruit, and place in casserole dish.

For the topping: In a separate medium bowl, combine flour, dark brown sugar *or* equivalent sweetener, salt, cinnamon, and ground ginger. Using two table knives or a pastry cutter, cut in the margarine until the mixture is coarse and crumbly.

Cover the filling evenly with the topping.

Bake 20 to 30 minutes or until the apricots have softened and topping is golden brown. Serve warm.

My Kid's **Allergic to Everything** *Dessert Cookbook*

Microwave Peach Crisp

This recipe, adapted from Chef Tyler Florence's family favorite, is so simple, yet so amazing.

Makes 4 to 6 servings

For the filling: In an ungreased 1½-quart microwave-safe casserole dish, combine peaches and brown sugar *or* equivalent sweetener.

For the topping: Place the cookies in a plastic bag. Using a rolling pin or a hammer or a soup can, crush the cookies. Add the walnuts to the crushed cookie mixture and shake to mix well. Add the oil to the nut and cookie mixture and knead bag to mix well. Sprinkle this topping over the peaches.

Microwave, loosely covered, on high for 3 minutes. Uncover the dish, rotate, and microwave on high for another 2 minutes. Cool for 20 to 25 minutes before serving.

FILLING

2 pounds peaches, pitted and sliced

2 tablespoons light *or* dark brown sugar, packed *or* equivalent sweetener

TOPPING

8 cinnamon *or* gingersnap cookies (see pages 108 and 110 for recipes)

2 tablespoons chopped walnuts

2 teaspoons mild tasting oil

Peach Crisp

FILLING
5 large peaches, pitted and sliced

1 tablespoon maple syrup *or* honey

1 tablespoon lemon juice

1 tablespoon oat flour

TOPPING
1 tablespoon oat flour

½ cup quick oats

¼ teaspoon salt

4 tablespoons maple syrup *or* honey

1 tablespoon mild tasting oil

1 tablespoon margarine

1 teaspoon vanilla extract, alcohol-free

Ripe, juicy, fuzzy peaches topped with oats and honey or crispy granola are perfect for summer.

Makes 4 to 6 servings

Preheat oven to 375°F. Use one ungreased 1½-quart casserole dish.

For the filling: In a medium bowl, toss the peaches with the maple syrup *or* honey, lemon juice, and flour, and spread evenly into casserole dish.

For the topping: In a separate small bowl, toss the flour, quick oats, and salt. In another small bowl, cream together the maple syrup *or* honey, oil, margarine, and vanilla. To this mixture, add the flour, oat, and salt mixture; mix well and sprinkle evenly over the peach filling.

Bake for 20 to 25 minutes, until peaches are bubbling and topping begins to brown.

Variation: Try 1½ cups granola (see page 141 for the recipe) instead of the topping.

*My Kid's **Allergic to Everything** Dessert Cookbook*

Microwave Plum Crumble

Fresh, ripe plums and honey are easily topped with oats mixed with cinnamon and nutmeg.

Makes 4 to 6 servings

For the filling: In a 1½-quart ungreased microwave-safe casserole dish, combine plums, honey, and arrowroot flour *or* potato starch.

For the topping: In a small bowl combine oats, brown sugar *or* equivalent sweetener, flour, cinnamon, and nutmeg. Using two table knives or a pastry cutter, cut the margarine into the mixture until coarse and crumbly. Sprinkle evenly over the filling.

Microwave on high for 6 to 7 minutes or until filling begins to bubble; rotate midway through cooking. Cool 20 to 30 minutes before serving.

FILLING
4 medium plums, pitted and sliced

2 tablespoons honey

2 tablespoons arrowroot flour *or* potato starch

TOPPING
3 tablespoons quick oats

3 tablespoons light *or* dark brown sugar, packed *or* equivalent sweetener

2 teaspoons oat flour

¼ teaspoon cinnamon

⅛ teaspoon nutmeg

1 tablespoon margarine

Rhubarb Strawberry Crumble

FILLING

1 pound rhubarb, cleaned and cut in ¼-inch pieces, strings removed

1 pint strawberries, cleaned, hulled, and halved

¾ cup sugar *or* equivalent sweetener

Grated peel of 1 orange

¼ cup orange juice

3 tablespoons arrowroot flour *or* kudzu powder

TOPPING

1 cup quick oats

⅓ cup oat flour

¼ cup light brown sugar, packed *or* equivalent sweetener

½ teaspoon cinnamon

½ cup chopped pecans *or* walnuts (optional)

5 tablespoons cold margarine

This classic, now revised, brings back sweet memories of my grandmother's kitchen; now my kids and I are making our own memories!

Makes 4 to 6 servings

Preheat oven to 350°F. Grease one 8-inch nonaluminum cake pan or baking dish.

For the filling: In a large bowl, mix rhubarb, strawberries, sugar *or* equivalent sweetener, orange peel, orange juice, and arrowroot powder *or* kudzu powder. Pour mixture into baking dish.

For the topping: In a small bowl mix oats, flour, brown sugar *or* equivalent sweetener, cinnamon, and nuts. Using two table knives or a pastry cutter, cut margarine into mixture until coarse and crumbly. Sprinkle over filling.

Bake for 45 to 50 minutes, until the fruit filling in the middle of the baking dish is thick and clear. Serve warm or cool.

My Kid's *Allergic to Everything* Dessert Cookbook

Apple Pandowdy

Every year we go apple picking and invite all our friends over to enjoy the bounty with us. This flavorful recipe is always a favorite.

Makes 6 to 8 servings

Preheat oven to 350°F. Use one ungreased 2½-quart casserole dish.

For the filling: In a large bowl, mix apples, sugar *or* equivalent sweetener, cinnamon, salt, and nutmeg. Place into casserole dish. In a separate bowl, mix maple syrup, water, and melted margarine *or* oil. Pour over apple mixture.

For the dough: In a separate medium bowl, mix flour, sugar *or* equivalent sweetener, and salt. Using two table knives or a pastry cutter, cut shortening *or* margarine *or* oil into flour mixture. Sprinkle in milk *or* ice water one tablespoonful at a time and knead until well mixed (the dough should clean off the sides of the bowl when rolled around). Shape the dough into a ball and place on a lightly floured surface. Roll out to fit snugly into the casserole dish.

Place the dough over the apple mixture and lightly brush the top of the dough with 2 tablespoons melted margarine *or* oil.

Bake for 30 minutes. Remove dish from oven, and using a sharp knife, cut the crust into small pieces, gently mixing the pieces into the apple filling. Return to oven and bake another 30 to 45 minutes or until apples are tender and crust pieces are golden brown. Serve hot or cold.

FILLING

6 medium apples, cored, peeled, and sliced

½ cup sugar *or* equivalent sweetener

½ teaspoon cinnamon

¼ teaspoon salt

¼ teaspoon nutmeg

½ cup maple syrup

3 tablespoons water

2 tablespoons melted margarine *or* mild tasting oil

DOUGH

1 cup flour (e.g., ½ cup oat and ½ cup barley; *or* see chart, pages 16–17)

2 tablespoons sugar *or* equivalent sweetener

¼ teaspoon salt

⅓ cup shortening *or* margarine *or* mild tasting oil

3 tablespoons ice water *or* allowable cold milk

2 tablespoons melted margarine *or* mild tasting oil

Pies and Tarts

What would childhood and summer be like without pie cooling in the kitchen? Or Thanksgiving without an apple or pumpkin pie for dessert? Pies are truly an American favorite and are perfect for any season. They are relatively easy to make and use fewer ingredients than most other desserts. You can use whatever fruits you have available. Though fresh, seasonal fruits are always best, frozen, canned, or dried fruits work well, too. The combinations of flavors and choices are endless, and your family will welcome these satisfying desserts year round.

Once you have explored the recipes in this chapter, you may be inspired to develop a few fillings uniquely your own. Enjoy!

Deep-Dish Apple-Rhubarb Pie

This recipe is very close to my mother's recipe. For me this is comfort food!

Makes one 10-inch deep-dish pie

CRUST
Dough for two 9-inch piecrusts, combined and rolled out to make one crust 18 inches across (the pastry crust works best with this pie: see page 70)

FILLING
¼ cup sugar *or* equivalent sweetener

¼ cup arrowroot flour

1 teaspoon cinnamon

4 large Granny Smith apples, cored and sliced into small wedges

2 tablespoons margarine

1 tablespoon lemon juice

2 pounds rhubarb stalks, cleaned and chopped into 1-inch pieces, strings removed

Prepare the pie dough according to directions. Roll out and set aside.

Preheat oven to 400°F. Use one ungreased 2½-quart casserole dish.

For the filling: In a large nonaluminum saucepan, combine sugar *or* equivalent sweetener, arrowroot flour, and cinnamon until well mixed. Stir in apples, margarine, and lemon juice; let sit for 5 minutes. Cover and cook over low heat on top of the stove until the apples begin to soften and the sauce begins to bubble, stirring occasionally. Remove from heat and stir in the rhubarb. Cool filling to room temperature.

Line the dish with the rolled-out dough, leaving dough hanging out over the rim. Mound the filling into the center of the crust, and bring the overhanging crust toward the middle of the filling, forming the dough into pleats or folds to allow it to lay flat on top of the filling. The center of the filling will be uncovered.

Place the casserole dish on a cookie sheet to catch drips as the pie bakes, and bake for 25 minutes. Lower oven temperature to 350°F, cover the pie with aluminum foil, and bake another 25 to 35 minutes, or until the filling begins to bubble up at the center. Cool and serve.

Banana Cream Pie

This delicious pie takes a few more steps, but it is worth it.
You won't be disappointed.

Makes one 9-inch pie

Prepare and bake the piecrust according to directions; set aside.

For the filling: Mix ¼ cup sugar *or* equivalent sweetener, flour, and salt in the top of a double boiler. Add milk and heat over a medium heat, stirring constantly until all of the sugar *or* equivalent sweetener and salt have dissolved. Cover and let cook for 15 minutes more, stirring occasionally.

In a separate bowl, beat the egg yolks with the remaining ¼ cup sugar *or* equivalent sweetener until creamy. Stir a little hot filling mixture from the double boiler into the yolk and sweetener mixture to warm it. Add the yolk and sweetener mixture to the filling mixture in the double boiler and cook for 2 more minutes over a medium heat, stirring constantly. Remove from heat and cool to room temperature.

When the filling has cooled, add the vanilla and stir in well. Spoon a thin layer of the filling into the baked pie crust. Top with a layer of sliced bananas. Spoon on another layer of filling, and add another layer of sliced bananas. Continue until all the filling and bananas are used. Chill in the refrigerator for at least one hour before serving.

Serve with nondairy whipped topping if desired.

CRUST
1 fully baked
9-inch piecrust
(see page 70)

FILLING
½ cup sugar
or equivalent
granulated
sweetener (such as
coconut sap sugar)

5 tablespoons
oat flour

½ teaspoon salt

2½ cups allowable
milk

3 egg yolks

1 teaspoon vanilla
extract, alcohol-free

3 bananas, sliced

Blueberry Pie

CRUST
Dough for one 9-inch piecrust (see page 70)

FILLING
2 pints blueberries, rinsed

⅓ cup margarine

1 cup dark brown sugar, packed *or* equivalent sweetener

½ teaspoon cinnamon

Grated peel of 1 lemon

½ cup lemon juice

⅓ cup arrowroot flour *or* kudzu powder

When we're lucky enough to get blueberries at the farmers market, this is my son's favorite!

Makes one 9-inch pie

Preheat oven to 400°F. Line one ungreased 9-inch pie pan with rolled-out pie dough.

For the filling: In a medium saucepan, mix the blueberries, margarine, brown sugar *or* equivalent sweetener, cinnamon, and lemon peel. Heat on top of the stove over medium heat, stirring constantly, until the berries are softened, approximately 5 minutes. In a small bowl, mix the lemon juice and arrowroot flour *or* kudzu powder until all lumps are dissolved. Add to the berry filling in the saucepan and stir over low to medium heat until the filling begins to thicken.

Remove the saucepan from heat and let the filling cool. When cooled, pour filling into the unbaked crust.

Place pie pan on a cookie sheet to catch any drips and bake for 45 minutes or until filling is bubbling. Serve warm or cool.

Cherry Pie

If you have never eaten a fresh cherry pie before, you are in for a treat. The flowery flavor of the cherries really comes through.

Makes one 9-inch pie

Prepare pie dough according to directions. Roll out.

Preheat oven to 450°F. Line one 9-inch pie pan with rolled-out dough.

For the filling: Mix cherries, sugar *or* equivalent sweetener, tapioca, and kirsch; let stand for 15 minutes. Pour fruit into unbaked piecrust and dot with margarine. If you are using a top crust, put it on over the filling. Be sure to crimp the edges to seal it and cut slits in the top to allow steam to escape.

Bake for 10 minutes, then reduce oven temperature to 350°F and continue baking another 40 minutes, until the edges of the crust are golden brown. Cool and serve.

CRUST
Dough for one 9-inch piecrust, *or* double the recipe if you want a top crust (see page 70)

FILLING
4 cups tart cherries, rinsed and pitted

⅓ cup sugar *or* equivalent sweetener

2 tablespoons plus 2 teaspoons quick-cooking tapioca

2 tablespoons kirsch, optional (cherry brandy liqueur)

2 tablespoons cold margarine

Nectarine Crumble Pie

The crumbly topping bakes to a nice golden color on this very attractive pie.

Makes one 9-inch pie

DOUGH
1 fully baked
9-inch piecrust
(see page 70)

FILLING
3 pounds ripe
nectarines, pitted
and sliced

⅔ cup sugar
or equivalent
sweetener

¼ cup any flour
containing gluten
(such as oat *or*
barley; *or* see chart,
page 7)

3 tablespoons
lemon juice

¼ teaspoon almond
or vanilla extract,
alcohol-free

TOPPING
⅔ cup flour (e.g.,
oat *or* spelt; *or* see
chart, page 15)

½ cup sugar
or granulated
sweetener (such as
coconut sap sugar)

½ cup chilled
margarine

Prepare and bake the piecrust according to directions; set aside.

Preheat oven to 450°F.

For the filling: In a large bowl, mix nectarines, sugar *or* equivalent sweetener, flour, lemon juice, and almond *or* vanilla extract, tossing well to completely coat the fruit. Spoon all the filling into cooked piecrust.

For the topping: In a small bowl, mix flour and sugar *or* sweetener. Using two table knives or a pastry cutter, cut the margarine into the mixture until mixture is coarse and crumbly. Sprinkle over the filling.

Bake for 15 minutes at 450°F; then reduce oven temperature to 350°F and bake for another 40 to 45 minutes. Cool and serve.

*My Kid's **Allergic to Everything** Dessert Cookbook*

Pumpkin Pie

Turn this old standby into a lesson on cooking creatively! Let kids smell the different spices and select different combinations each time you make it.

Makes one 9-inch pie

Prepare and bake the piecrust according to directions; set aside.

Preheat oven to 350°F.

For the filling: In a large bowl, mix the pumpkin with the sugar *or* equivalent sweetener, salt, spices and vanilla. Beat in the egg yolks *or* Ener-G Egg Replacer powder mixture and milk.

Pour the pumpkin mixture into the piecrust. If you are using a dough crust, cover the edges of the crust with foil so it doesn't burn.

Bake 30 minutes, or until a toothpick inserted in the center comes out clean.

Cool and serve.

DOUGH
1 fully baked
9-inch piecrust
(see page 70)

FILLING
1½ cups cooked
mashed pumpkin

⅔ cup date sugar
or equivalent
sweetener

½ teaspoon salt

1 teaspoon
cinnamon

½ teaspoon nutmeg

½ teaspoon ginger

½ teaspoon cloves

½ teaspoon vanilla
extract, alcohol-free

2 egg yolks *or* 3
teaspoons Ener-G
Egg Replacer
powder mixed with
4 tablespoons water

½ cup allowable
milk

Shoofly Pie

CRUST
Dough for one
9-inch piecrust
(see page 70)

FILLING
½ cup any flour
containing gluten
(such as oat *or*
amaranth; see
chart, page 7)

1 cup light *or*
dark brown
sugar, packed
or equivalent
sweetener

⅛ teaspoon salt

4 tablespoons cold
margarine

2 teaspoons baking
soda

½ cup light
molasses

A gooey pie made with brown sugar and molasses, Shoofly Pie is a traditional favorite among the Amish and Pennsylvania Dutch. Maybe it will become one of yours, too.

Makes one 9-inch pie

Prepare the pie dough according to directions. Roll out.

Preheat oven to 350°F. Line one 9-inch pie pan with rolled-out dough.

Combine flour, brown sugar *or* equivalent sweetener, salt, and margarine. Mix only until crumbly; do not overmix. In a small saucepan, dissolve the baking soda and molasses on top of the stove over a very low heat. Add ¾ of the crumbly mixture to the saucepan and mix well. Pour this into the pie pan. Sprinkle the remaining ¼ of the crumbly mixture over the top.

Bake for 30 minutes or until the center is firm. Serve slightly warm or cold.

Very Berry Pie

This is a warm, melt-in-your-mouth pie perfect for company.

Makes one 9-inch pie

Prepare the pie dough according to directions. Roll out.

Preheat oven to 400°F. Line one 9-inch pie pan with one rolled-out dough crust and reserve second dough for the top crust.

For the filling: Toss berries with lemon juice, flour, sugar *or* equivalent sweetener, tapioca, and salt. Let stand for 20 minutes. Place the berry filling in the crust in the pie pan and dot with margarine. Place the second crust on top, crimping the edges to seal; cut slits in the top to allow steam to escape

Bake approximately 45 minutes or until the crust is deep brown and the filling is bubbly. Let pie cool at least 2 hours to allow the juices to thicken before serving.

To serve slightly warm, reheat at 300°F for 15 minutes.

CRUST
Dough for two 9-inch pie pans (the dough crust works best; see page 70)

FILLING
9 cups mixed cleaned berries, any combination*

1 tablespoon lemon juice

1 tablespoon any mild tasting flour (such as oat, millet *or* soy)

⅔ to 1 cup sugar *or* equivalent sweetener to taste

¼ cup quick-cooking small pearl tapioca

1 pinch salt

2 tablespoons cold margarine

*You can use 4 cups of mixed berries to make a delicious but much lower pie if you don't have 9 cups of berries on hand; just reduce the sweetener to ½ cup. Also, wild organic blueberries are much tarter than strawberries, so you may want more sweetener.

Vim and Vinegar Pie

CRUST
1 fully baked 9-inch piecrust (the dough crust works best; see page 70)

FILLING
8 tablespoons margarine

2 tablespoons any mild tasting flour (such as oat, barley, millet, *or* soy)

1 cup dark brown sugar, packed

½ cup sugar *or* equivalent sweetener

4 egg yolks *or* 4½ teaspoons Ener-G Egg Replacer powder

¼ cup apple juice

¼ cup cider vinegar

¼ cup chopped walnuts *or* pecans (optional)

Vinegar pies were popular all over the Midwest. Lemons were scarce and expensive so vinegar was substituted. Using apple juice along with apple cider vinegar gives it a delicious apple taste.

Makes one 9-inch pie

Prepare and bake the piecrust according to directions; set aside.

Preheat oven to 375°F.

For the filling: In a medium bowl, cream together the margarine, flour, brown sugar, and sugar *or* equivalent sweetener. Add the egg yolks *or* Ener-G Egg Replacer powder and beat well, until fluffy. Stir in apple juice and vinegar until blended. Pour into baked piecrust. If using nuts, sprinkle them on top.

Bake for 50 to 60 minutes, or until an inserted toothpick comes out clean. Cool before serving.

My Kid's *Allergic to Everything* Dessert Cookbook

Apple-Raisin Tart

The addition of raisins transforms this good but basic apple pie into an exceptional treat.

Makes one 11-inch tart *or* one 9-inch pie

Prepare the pie dough according to directions. Roll out.

Preheat oven to 400°F. Line one 11-inch tart pan *or* one 9-inch pie pan with rolled-out dough.

For the filling: In a medium bowl, mix apples, lemon juice, and raisins well. Add sugar *or* equivalent sweetener, flour, cinnamon, and nutmeg; combine well. Spread evenly over the dough.

Bake for 40 to 50 minutes, until the edges of the pastry are well browned and apple edges begin to brown. Cool slightly.

This may be served with a whipped topping.

CRUST
Dough for one
9-inch piecrust
(see page 70)

FILLING
6 medium cooking
apples, peeled,
cored, and sliced

1 tablespoon
lemon juice

½ cup raisins

1 cup sugar
or equivalent
sweetener

½ tablespoon any
mild tasting flour
(such as soy, millet,
barley, *or* oat)

1 teaspoon
cinnamon

¼ teaspoon nutmeg

Pear Tart

This tart is an attractive, delicious way to use pears of any sort. Pears tend to keep their shape, making these individual tarts very appealing.

Makes 6 tarts

CRUST
Dough for one 9-inch piecrust (see page 70)

FILLING
¼ cup margarine

½ cup light *or* dark brown sugar, packed *or* equivalent sweetener

1 tablespoon brandy *or* dark rum

1 teaspoon lemon juice

¼ teaspoon cinnamon

2 large pears, peeled, quartered, and cored

Prepare the pie dough according to directions. Roll out and set aside.

Preheat oven to 375°F. Use one large ungreased cookie sheet.

For the filling: In a large frying pan, melt margarine over medium heat on top of the stove. Add the sugar *or* equivalent sweetener, brandy *or* rum, lemon juice, and cinnamon; stir over medium heat until the sugar dissolves. Slice each pear quarter lengthwise into 4 even slices and add to the liquid in the frying pan. Poach the pear slices gently until tender, about 8 to 10 minutes.

Using a slotted spoon, remove the pear slices to a plate and set them aside. Heat the liquid in the frying pan over a high heat until it is reduced to a thick bubbling syrup, about 1 minute. Set aside.

Place the rolled-out pie dough on a lightly floured board. Using the tip of a sharp knife, cut out 6 whole pear-shaped pieces, approximately 3 by 5 inches each. Place the pastry shapes on an ungreased cookie sheet. Arrange 5 pear slices on top of each shape, fanning pieces to resemble a whole pear, and leave a small border of pastry around slices. Fit the 2 remaining slices onto any two pastry shapes, or eat them. Brush the reduced syrup on top of the pear slices.

Bake 10 to 15 minutes or until pastry is golden brown. Serve warm or cooled.

Monstrously Delicious Cookies

After much experimentation, we discovered that the insulated, double-layer "never burn" cookie sheets are well worth the money! If you don't have a set or don't want to spend the money, try using two regular cookie sheets, one right on top of the other. Because using alternative flours and ingredients results in cookie doughs that are not as "sticky" as those made from bleached, enriched wheat flour, our cookie doughs spread as they heat up; a regular cookie sheet tends to allow the dough to heat too rapidly and almost fry onto the sheet before it can bake.

Baking one sheet of cookies at a time, placed in the middle of the center rack in the oven, allows the heat to circulate more evenly.

A slightly lower oven temperature allows the dough to bake thoroughly while lessening the chance of having edges or bottoms burn.

Finally, chilling the dough by shoving the bowl right into the refrigerator between forming each batch of cookies, and also allowing the cookie sheets to cool thoroughly before baking the next batch, helps keep the dough more firm while it bakes.

In each recipe's list of ingredients, we have put the ingredient which works best first, e.g., oat flour *or* spelt flour *or* amaranth flour. This means we have achieved the tastiest results with oat flour, but have also been successful using the other flours. If there is only one ingredient listed in a line, this means we have not found (or do not need) any alternatives.

The Cookie Flour Chart on pages 18–19 in chapter 1 will help guide you in your flour selections.

Aaron's Honey Barley Cookies

½ cup honey

⅓ cup mild tasting oil (coconut, canola, etc.)

1¼ cups barley flour

½ teaspoon baking powder

¼ teaspoon baking soda

¼ teaspoon salt

½ teaspoon vanilla extract, alcohol-free

We also enjoy this with ½ cup of dried, cut up fruit or carob chips mixed in.

Makes 2 dozen cookies

Preheat oven to 325°F. Grease 2 cookie sheets and chill.

In a large bowl, combine all ingredients and mix well. Drop the dough by teaspoonfuls onto the greased cookie sheets. Place one cookie sheet in the oven, centered on the middle rack. Chill the other cookie sheet until the first batch is baked.

Bake for 12 to 15 minutes, or until the cookies begin to turn golden brown. Cool on the cookie sheets.

Bird's Nest Cookies

These thumbprint cookies are rolled in chopped nuts and look like little bird's nests. The combination of the cookie and the gooey filling makes a wonderful treat.

Makes 2 dozen cookies

Preheat oven to 350°F. Lightly grease cookie sheet.

Cream the margarine *or* shortening with the sugar, egg yolk, and almond extract until smooth and almost fluffy. Fold in the flour and mix well. Place the chopped nuts in a shallow bowl and set aside. Form the dough into small balls, approximately ½-inch in size, then roll each ball in the chopped nuts. Place the coated balls on the greased cookie sheet and bake for 7 to 8 minutes.

Remove the cookie sheet from the oven and make a deep depression in the center of each cookie ball with your thumb or the tip of a spoon, being careful to not go all the way through the cookie to the sheet. Spoon a teaspoonful of jam, jelly, or preserves into the depression and return the cookie sheet to the oven to bake for another 8 minutes.

½ cup softened allowable margarine *or* shortening

¼ cup brown sugar, packed *or* date sugar

1 egg yolk *or* ¼ teaspoon Ener-G Egg Replacer powder mixed with 1 teaspoon water

½ teaspoon almond extract, alcohol-free

1 cup flour (e.g., ¾ cup oat *or* spelt and ¼ cup barley *or* millet; *or* see chart, pages 18–19)

1 cup finely chopped allowable nuts, any type

Approximately ½ cup jam, jelly, or preserves, any flavor (see chapter 10) for fillings

Carrot Cookies

1 cup any sticky
flours (see page 7)

1 teaspoon baking
powder

¼ teaspoon salt

½ cup sugar
or equivalent
sweetener

2 egg yolks *or* ½
teaspoon Ener-G
Egg Replacer
powder mixed with
1½ teaspoons water

½ cup allowable
shortening
or allowable
margarine *or*
mild tasting oil
(safflower *or*
canola, etc.)

½ cup steamed and
mashed carrots

*These cookies have a smooth texture, delicious flavor,
and are great for a picky eater.*

Makes approximately 2 dozen cookies

Preheat oven to 400°F. Grease cookie sheet.

Combine the flour, baking powder, salt, and sugar *or* equivalent sweetener. Add the egg yolks *or* Ener-G Egg Replacer powder mixture, allowable shortening *or* margarine *or* oil, and carrots. Mix until well blended. Drop by teaspoonfuls onto greased cookie sheet. Place cookie sheet centered on the middle rack.

Bake for 8 minutes. Cool cookies on cookie sheet.

Chocolate Drop Cookies

Fill your cookie jar with these easy-to-make cookies that are always a big hit.

Makes 3 dozen small cookies

Preheat oven to 375°F. Use ungreased cookie sheet.

In a large bowl, beat the sugar *or* equivalent sweetener, margarine, egg yolk *or* Ener-G Egg Replacer powder mixture, and almond *or* vanilla extract until fluffy. Stir in the carob *or* cocoa powder and beat again until fluffy. Stir in the flours ½ cup at a time, mixing well after each addition. By teaspoonfuls, drop the dough onto the cookie sheet, leaving 1 inch between cookies.

Bake for 6 to 8 minutes. Using a spatula, place the cookies immediately on a platter for cooling.

½ cup sugar *or* equivalent sweetener

¾ cup softened margarine

1 egg yolk *or* ¼ teaspoon Ener-G Egg Replacer powder mixed with 1 teaspoon water

1 teaspoon almond extract *or* vanilla extract, alcohol-free

¼ cup carob powder *or* cocoa powder

1½ cups any sticky flours (see page 7)

Cinnamon Crispies

⅓ cup mild tasting oil *or* softened margarine

⅓ cup maple syrup

⅓ cup allowable yogurt, plain, vanilla, *or* maple flavor

1 teaspoon baking soda

1 teaspoon cinnamon

¾ cup any sticky flours (see page 7)

This delicate cookie has become a family favorite.

Makes approximately 2 dozen cookies

Preheat oven to 350°F. Grease and flour cookie sheet.

Cream together the oil *or* margarine, maple syrup, and yogurt until smooth. Add the baking soda and cinnamon; beat well. Add the flour and beat until almost fluffy. Drop the batter by teaspoonfuls onto cookie sheet, leaving 2½ inches between cookies.

Bake for 10 minutes, or until the cookie edges begin to turn golden. Cool on the cookie sheet, then place the cookies on a platter, carefully lifting each cookie with a spatula. Cookies will become crisp as they cool to room temperature. You may also refrigerate them to crisp more quickly.

Sunny Citrus Cookies

When lemons are in season I put fresh lemon zest and lemon juice in ice cube trays in the freezer to have handy when I want to have a taste of these sunshine cookies in the middle of winter.

Makes 21 cookies

Preheat oven to 350°F. Line a cookie sheet with parchment paper.

Combine vegetable shortening, coconut sap sugar, and granulated sugar in a medium bowl and mix with an electric mixer for 1 minute. Scrape side of bowl and mix for one more minute. Mixture will start to look creamy. Add Ener-G Egg Replacer powder mixture and beat well. Add in lemon zest and juice, and vanilla and orange extracts. Scrape side of bowl again. Add flours and guar gum and mix until well combined. Batter will be creamy. Drop scant teaspoonfuls of dough onto prepared cookie sheet.

Bake 12 to 13 minutes until cookies are slightly brown around the edges. Loosen cookies on cookie sheet with spatula, and cool on wire racks before eating.

¼ cup vegetable shortening

¼ cup coconut sap sugar

½ cup granulated white sugar

1 tablespoon Ener-G Egg Replacer powder vigorously mixed with 4 tablespoons water

1 teaspoon lemon zest (about ½ medium lemon)

1 tablespoon freshly squeezed lemon juice (about ½ medium lemon)

½ teaspoon vanilla extract, alcohol-free

½ teaspoon orange extract, alcohol-free

½ cup oat flour

¼ cup quinoa flour

3 tablespoons brown rice flour

¼ teaspoon guar gum

Gingersnaps

¾ cup softened margarine

1 cup sugar *or* equivalent sweetener*

¼ cup dark brown sugar, packed *or* date sugar

1 egg yolk *or* ¼ teaspoon Ener-G Egg Replacer powder mixed with 1 teaspoon water

2 teaspoons baking soda

1 teaspoon ground cloves

1 teaspoon ginger

1 teaspoon cinnamon

¼ teaspoon salt

2½ cups any sticky flours (see page 7)

*Note: For a darker and richer taste, substitute ½ cup molasses for ½ cup of the sugar or equivalent sweetener.

I always kick off the holiday season with a double batch of these gingersnap cookies. It has become our family tradition.

Makes approximately 2 dozen cookies

Preheat oven to 325°F. Use ungreased cookie sheet.

In a large bowl, cream the margarine, sugar *or* equivalent sweetener, egg yolk *or* Ener-G Egg Replacer powder mixture, and brown *or* date sugar together until fluffy. Add baking soda, cloves, ginger, cinnamon, and salt, beating again until fluffy. Add the flour, ½ cup at a time, mixing well after each addition. Drop the dough by generous teaspoonfuls onto the cookie sheet and very slightly flatten each cookie with the palm of your hand.

Bake 12 to 15 minutes, or until the cookie edges become golden brown. Cool the cookies on the cookie sheet.

Gluten-Free Orange Snaps

These bite-size citrus cookies are always a big hit.

Makes 5 dozen cookies

Preheat oven to 375°F. Line cookie sheets with parchment paper.

In electric mixer bowl, cream together oil, shortening, brown sugar, and granulated sugar. Add orange juice and orange zest to Ener-G Egg Replacer powder mixture and mix well. Beat into creamed mixture. In separate bowl combine flour with baking soda, salt, baking powder, and guar gum and mix well. Add flour mixture slowly to creamed mixture. Put in refrigerator until firm enough to handle, about an hour.

Roll dough into logs about 1½ inches in diameter and roll up in waxed paper. Chill again in refrigerator until very cold and firm.

When firm, cut into ¼ inch slices and put on prepared cookie sheets, leaving room for cookies to spread during baking. Bake at 375°F for 12 to 15 minutes.

¼ cup coconut oil

¼ cup vegetable shortening

¼ cup brown sugar, packed

¼ cup white granulated sugar

1½ teaspoons Ener-G Egg Replacer powder mixed vigorously with 2 tablespoons water

1 tablespoon fresh squeezed orange juice

1½ teaspoon orange zest

1⅓ cups Bob's Red Mill Gluten Free All Purpose Baking Flour

¼ teaspoon guar gum

½ teaspoon baking soda

¼ teaspoon salt

¼ teaspoon baking powder

Hamentashen Cookies

½ cup allowable shortening *or* margarine *or* coconut cream (the thick part at the top of the can), softened

⅔ cup sugar *or* equivalent granulated sweetener

¼ teaspoon Ener-G Egg Replacer powder mixed with 2 teaspoons water

2 tablespoons allowable milk

1 teaspoon vanilla extract, alcohol-free

2¾ cups any sticky flours (see page 7)

2 teaspoons baking powder

½ cup any jam, jelly, or preserves (see chapter 10)

For Purim, we dress up these cookies with a variety of fillings.

Makes approximately 2 dozen cookies

Preheat oven to 375°F. Grease 2 cookie sheets and chill.

In a large bowl, cream together the allowable shortening *or* margarine, sugar *or* equivalent sweetener, Ener-G Egg Replacer powder mixture, allowable milk, and vanilla extract until well mixed. Slowly add the flour, ½ cup at a time, until well mixed. Add the baking powder and mix well.

Roll the dough out on a floured surface until it is approximately ¼ inch thick. Using a round cookie cutter or water glass, cut out as many circles as you can. Place several on one cookie sheet. Place a teaspoonful of jam, jelly, or preserves in the center of each circle, and bring up the sides in three parts to make a triangle shape. Pinch the tops of the three corners until they hold together. Continue making hamentashen until the cookie sheets are filled, but the cookies are not touching. Return one filled cookie sheet to the fridge to chill.

Bake for 15 minutes on the center rack in the center of the oven, or until lightly browned. Let cool on the sheets.

Jacob's Drizzle Drop Cookies

Try these tasty, crispy cookies topped with a sprinkle of luscious carob chips.

Makes approximately 3 dozen cookies

Preheat oven to 350°F. Grease cookie sheet.

For the cookies: Cream together all the cookie ingredients except the oat bran *or* oats. Once the dough is well blended and airy, stir in the oat bran *or* oats. Do not over mix. The dough is crumbly but will bake solid cookies. Drop the dough by teaspoonfuls onto the cookie sheet, leaving 2 inches between cookies.

Bake 4 to 6 minutes, or until the edges become golden brown. Once the edges have browned, remove the cookies from the oven and let them cool on the cookie sheet for 2 minutes, then remove them from the cookie sheets and place them on a large platter in a single layer.

For the topping: In a large saucepan, melt the carob *or* chocolate chips and the margarine over a low heat on top of the stove, stirring constantly. Once the chips are completely melted, drizzle the topping over the cooled cookies with a spoon. Refrigerate the cookies to set the chocolate drizzle topping.

COOKIE

½ cup sugar *or* equivalent sweetener

1 pinch salt

½ cup softened margarine

½ teaspoon vanilla extract, alcohol-free

½ teaspoon almond extract, alcohol-free

1 rounded teaspoon arrowroot flour mixed with ¼ cup water

1½ cups oat bran *or* quick oats

DRIZZLE TOPPING

¼ cup semisweet carob chips *or* chocolate chips

2 tablespoons margarine

Josh's Chocolate Chip Cookies

Josh was six years old when I first made these. I packed them in a Famous Amos bag (well cleaned out!) so he had cookies "just like the other kids" for his birthday treat at school.

Makes 3 dozen cookies

Preheat oven to 350°F. Use ungreased cookie sheets.

Cream together allowable shortening *or* margarine, vanilla, brown sugar *or* date sugar, and sugar *or* equivalent sweetener. Add egg yolks *or* Ener-G Egg Replacer powder and cream well. Add salt and baking powder; mix well. Add the flour, ½ cup at a time, mixing well after each addition. After all the flour is mixed in, stir in the chips.

Place one tablespoonful of dough in the palm of your hand and gently form a ball. Still using the palm of your hand, lightly press the dough onto the cookie sheet but do not flatten it! Leave approximately 2 inches between the balls of dough.

Bake for 11 to 12 minutes or until the cookies flatten somewhat and the edges begin to turn golden brown. Cool the cookies on the cookie sheet; after they have cooled, use a spatula to move them to a platter.

1 cup softened allowable shortening *or* softened margarine

1 teaspoon vanilla extract, alcohol-free

1 cup brown sugar, packed *or* date sugar

1 cup sugar *or* equivalent sweetener

2 egg yolks *or* 3 teaspoons Ener-G Egg Replacer powder

½ teaspoon salt

1 teaspoon baking powder

2¼ cups any sticky flours (see page 7)

12 ounces carob *or* chocolate chips (mini chips or regular size)

*My Kid's **Allergic to Everything** Dessert Cookbook*

Oatmeal Cookies

We brought these cookies to my son's school and no one guessed that they were made with allergy-free ingredients.

Makes approximately 2 dozen cookies

Preheat oven to 375°F. Grease cookie sheets.

In a large bowl, cream margarine *or* shortening, brown sugar *or* date sugar, egg yolk *or* Ener-G Egg Replacer powder mixture, milk, and vanilla until fluffy. Add oats, flour, baking soda, salt, and cinnamon. Beat again until well mixed. Stir in raisins and nuts, if desired.

Drop by tablespoonfuls onto cookie sheets and bake for 10 to 12 minutes or until cookies are lightly browned. Cool on cookie sheets.

¾ cup softened margarine **or** softened allowable shortening

¼ cup brown sugar, packed **or** date sugar

1 egg yolk **or** ¼ teaspoon Ener-G Egg Replacer powder mixed with 1 teaspoon water

⅓ cup allowable milk

½ teaspoon vanilla extract, alcohol-free

3 cups quick oats

1 cup any sticky flours (see page 7)

½ teaspoon baking soda

½ teaspoon salt

¼ teaspoon cinnamon

1 cup raisins (optional)

1 cup chopped nuts (optional)

Scones

My Celtic heritage compelled me to create this recipe, and the kids love it!

Makes 8 scones

2 cups oat flour

¼ cup granulated sugar *or* equivalent sweetener

1½ teaspoons baking powder

½ teaspoon baking soda

¼ teaspoon salt

2 teaspoons lemon zest (about 1 lemon)

¼ cup margarine *or* allowable shortening, chilled and cut into ¼ inch pieces

1½ teaspoons Ener-G Egg Replacer powder vigorously beaten with 2 tablespoons water

2 tablespoons lemon juice (about 1 lemon)

½ cup oat milk

Preheat oven to 400°F. Line a cookie sheet with parchment paper.

In a large bowl, mix the flour, sugar *or* equivalent sweetener, baking powder, baking soda, and salt. Stir in the lemon zest. Using two table knives or a pastry cutter, cut in the margarine *or* shortening until the dough is mealy. Blend in the Ener-G Egg Replacer powder mixture and the lemon juice. Stir in just enough oat milk to make the dough sticky.

Plop the dough onto a floured surface and knead it gently until the dough comes together (about 5 or 6 kneads). Pat the dough into an 8-inch mound. Cut the mound into 8 wedges. Place the wedges on the parchment paper, making sure they don't touch.

Bake about 15 to 20 minutes, or until the scones are golden and crusty. Serve warm. May serve with jam, jelly, or preserves (see chapter 10).

My Kid's *Allergic to Everything* Dessert Cookbook

Sugar Cookies

Fabulous sugar cookies are easy to make and perfect to decorate for any occasion.
Makes 18 to 24 cookies

Preheat oven to 375°F. Grease cookie sheets.

In a large bowl, cream margarine, sugar *or* equivalent sweetener, and milk until well mixed. Beat in egg yolk *or* Ener-G Egg Replacer powder mixture and vanilla until fluffy. Add salt and baking powder, beating again until fluffy. Add flour, ½ cup at a time, and mix well after each addition. Chill the dough for 30 minutes or more in refrigerator. Drop the dough by tablespoonfuls onto the cookie sheet, leaving at least 2 inches between cookies.

Bake for 7 to 9 minutes in the middle of the center rack, or until cookie edges begin to turn golden brown. Cool on cookie sheet.

½ cup softened margarine

¾ cup sugar *or* equivalent sweetener

1 tablespoon soy milk *or* rice milk *or* almond milk

1 egg yolk *or* ¼ teaspoon Ener-G Egg Replacer powder mixed with 1 teaspoon water

½ teaspoon vanilla extract, alcohol-free

¼ teaspoon salt

¼ teaspoon baking powder

1¼ cup flours (see pages 18–19)

Toffee Squares

4½ cups quick oats

¼ cup brown sugar, packed *or* date sugar

¾ cup melted margarine

½ cup agave inulin powder, vanilla flavored

1 tablespoon coconut milk

1 tablespoon vanilla extract, alcohol-free

½ teaspoon salt

12 ounces carob chips *or* chocolate chips

½ cup sliced almonds (optional)

A strong toffee flavor makes these a delightful treat.

Preheat oven to 400°F. Grease one 13 by 9-inch baking pan.

Mix the oats, brown sugar *or* date sugar, margarine, agave inulin powder, coconut milk, vanilla, and salt very well. Press the mixture firmly into the baking pan.

Bake for 15 minutes or until the mixture becomes bubbly. Remove the pan from the oven and turn the oven off. Immediately sprinkle carob *or* chocolate chips over the top and return the pan to the oven until the chips are completely melted (up to several minutes). After the chips have melted, remove the pan from the oven and cool for ten minutes. Then sprinkle on the almonds and lightly press them into the carob or chocolate topping. Cool completely, cut into squares, and serve.

Tropical Fruit Bars

These are a nice holiday treat to make and share with friends. They are much more mouthwatering than anything you can purchase in a store!

Preheat oven to 350°F. Grease one 9 by 13-inch baking dish.

For the filling: In a medium saucepan, simmer the dates, vanilla, and pineapple until the mixture begins to thicken, stirring occasionally. Once it begins to thicken, remove the filling from the heat and set aside.

For the base: In a medium bowl, combine the flour, coconut, nuts, oats, and brown sugar *or* date sugar, and mix well. Add the orange juice and margarine *or* allowable shortening *or* coconut cream *or* oil and mix thoroughly. Press half of this base mixture into the baking dish. Pour all of the filling evenly over this base. Spread the remaining half of the base mixture evenly over the filling.

Bake for 30 to 40 minutes, until the top crust is golden brown.

Cool in the baking dish, then slice into squares and serve.

FILLING

2 cups chopped pitted dates

1 tablespoon vanilla extract, alcohol-free

2½ cups unsweetened crushed pineapple, with juice

BASE

1 cup oat flour

1 cup unsweetened shredded coconut

½ cup chopped pecans *or* walnuts

3 cups quick oats

¼ cup brown sugar, packed *or* date sugar

1 cup orange juice

¼ cup softened margarine *or* softened allowable shortening *or* softened coconut cream (the thick white part at the top of the can) *or* mild tasting oil

Doughnut Holes

3 cups oil (for frying)

4 cups flours (any mostly sticky combination, such as 3 cups oat *or* spelt and 1 cup barley *or* millet; see page 7)

1 teaspoon salt

1 teaspoon any one *or* combination of dried ground nutmeg, cinnamon, allspice, and cloves

1 tablespoon baking powder

3 tablespoons club soda

1 tablespoon honey

⅓ cup melted allowable shortening *or* melted margarine *or* mild tasting oil

1 cup soy milk *or* rice milk *or* almond milk *or* water

Fill your craving for doughnut holes with these delectable tidbits.

Makes approximately 2 dozen

In a deep fryer or large saucepan, heat 3 cups oil to 375°F.

In a large bowl, combine the flour, salt, and spices. Mix the baking powder with club soda. Mix with honey, allowable shortening *or* margarine *or* oil, and milk *or* water; mix until the dough is well blended and smooth.

Drop the dough by single teaspoonfuls into the hot oil and fry until the doughnut holes are golden brown. Do not crowd them; fry only a few at one time.

Remove the doughnut holes with a slotted metal spoon and drain on paper towels. May serve warm or cooled.

*My Kid's **Allergic to Everything** Dessert Cookbook*

Energy Balls

These treats will last several weeks if refrigerated.

Makes 2 to 3 dozen

In a large bowl, combine the milk powder, granola, oat bran, and coconut. Mash in the nut butter and the honey until all ingredients are well mixed. Shape into 1-inch balls, place on a serving platter, cover and chill for several hours before serving.

½ cup Better Than Milk powder *or* goat's milk powder, unreconstituted

½ cup granola (see page 141)

½ cup oat bran

⅔ cup coconut flakes *or* shredded coconut

1 cup nut *or* seed butter (e.g., tahini, sunflower, almond, *or* cashew)

½ cup honey

Special Desserts

9

Once in a while, the urge overwhelms you to create a sensational dessert that will knock your family's socks off! Try these recipes when winter chill begins creeping in the kitchen door, or when company is coming for Sunday dinner and it is too hot to bake a cake. No need to worry that your child will feel awkward or left out because he or she cannot share that special dessert.

Your choices range from custard to mousse to pudding. We also have a versatile shortbread that may be served as a dessert cookie or topped with fruit and used as short-cake. Serve sherbet or sorbet for a cool ending to hot summer days, and our tapioca will warm anyone's heart any time of year.

We guarantee that at least one of these desserts will allow you to dance from the kitchen bearing a treat that will make their eyes light up and their lips go "Ooooooh!"

Sweet Potato Custard

2 cups peeled, baked, and mashed sweet potatoes *or* yams

16 ounces medium *or* soft tofu, drained and uncooked

3 tablespoons orange juice *or* apple juice concentrate, undiluted

½ cup margarine

5 egg yolks *or* 6 teaspoons Ener-G Egg Replacer powder mixed with 4 teaspoons water

2 teaspoons lemon zest (1 medium lemon)

1 teaspoon cinnamon

½ teaspoon nutmeg

¼ teaspoon allspice

¼ teaspoon ground clove

1 teaspoon vanilla extract, alcohol-free*

½ cup soy *or* rice milk

*Note: If vanilla-flavored soy milk *or* rice milk is used, reduce the vanilla to ½ teaspoon.

This dessert gets its mild sweetness from the sweet potatoes and juice—no need for extra sweetener!

Makes 4 to 6 servings

Preheat oven to 350°F. Use one ungreased 1½-quart baking or casserole dish.

Combine all the ingredients in a blender or food processor and mix until the batter is completely smooth and free of lumps. Pour the batter into the baking or casserole dish and bake for 1 hour or until an inserted table knife comes out clean.

Chill well before serving. Scoop into pretty serving bowls; may be topped with nondairy whipped topping.

Quick Chocolate Mousse

Use your blender to whip up this easy, creamy chocolate mousse recipe.

Makes 2 servings

In separate small saucepans, heat the coffee and milk to almost boiling. The liquid must be hot enough to melt the carob *or* chocolate and to cook the egg yolk in order for the mousse to set well.

Pour the coffee and milk into a blender. Add carob chips *or* chocolate chips and dark rum. Blend on the high setting for 3 seconds. Add the egg yolk *or* Ener-G Egg Replacer powder mixture and blend on the high setting for another 2 minutes.

Pour the mousse into 2 individual dessert dishes and chill for 6 to 8 hours.

2 tablespoons strong coffee

¾ cup soy milk *or* almond milk

6 ounces carob chips *or* chocolate chips

3 tablespoons dark rum

1 egg yolk *or* ½ teaspoon Ener-G Egg Replacer powder mixed with ½ teaspoon water

Brownie Pudding

This very rich and chocolatey dessert was a huge hit with my family.

Makes 4 to 6 servings

1 cup any sticky flours (see page 7)

½ cup sugar *or* equivalent sweetener

6 tablespoons unsweetened carob powder *or* cocoa powder, divided in half

2 teaspoons baking powder

½ teaspoon salt

½ cup soy milk *or* rice milk *or* almond milk

2 tablespoons mild tasting oil

1 teaspoon vanilla extract, alcohol-free

½ cup finely chopped nuts (optional)

½ cup dark brown sugar, packed *or* date sugar

¼ cup water

Preheat oven to 350°F. Lightly grease one 8-inch square baking pan.

In a medium bowl, combine the flour, sugar *or* equivalent sweetener, 3 tablespoons of the carob powder *or* cocoa powder, baking powder, and salt; mix well. Add the milk, oil, and vanilla; beat until smooth. Fold in the nuts, if using. Pour the batter into the baking pan.

In a separate small bowl, mix the brown sugar *or* date sugar and the remaining 3 tablespoons carob powder *or* cocoa powder. Sprinkle this over the batter.

In a small saucepan, heat the water just until hot and pour it over the batter in the baking pan.

Bake for 45 minutes or until the pudding top begins to get crusty and the bottom layer begins to thicken.

Serve warm or cool.

Marbled Chocolate Pudding

This creamy pudding is one of my family's comfort foods. We always make it for family gatherings.

Makes 4 servings

In a medium saucepan, combine sugar *or* equivalent sweetener, arrowroot flour, salt, and milk; heat over medium heat on top of the stove, stirring until smooth. Reduce the heat to low and stir in the unsweetened chocolate *or* carob, stirring constantly until the chocolate *or* carob is melted and the pudding begins to thicken.

Remove the saucepan from the heat and slowly add the egg yolks, stirring constantly to prevent clotting. Return the saucepan to medium heat and stir for another 2 minutes.

Remove the saucepan from the heat and pour the pudding into a medium bowl. Cover it with plastic wrap and let the pudding cool for 5 minutes, then stir in the white chocolate just until it has blended in. Keep the pudding in this bowl or pour into individual dessert bowls. May serve warm, or let it cool in the refrigerator before serving.

Note: This may also be prepared in your microwave in a large microwave-safe bowl. Microwave on high for 2 to 4 minutes each time the recipe says to heat on the stove, and stir after each minute.

½ cup sugar *or* equivalent sweetener

2½ tablespoons arrowroot flour

⅛ teaspoon salt

2 cups soy milk *or* almond milk

2 ounces unsweetened chocolate *or* carob, coarsely chopped

3 egg yolks, beaten

2 ounces white chocolate (if allowable), finely chopped

Creamy Rice Pudding

3 cups oat milk

3 cups cooked white rice

3 teaspoons stevia powder

2 teaspoons vanilla extract, alcohol-free **or** seeds from 1 vanilla pod

¼ teaspoon salt

1 teaspoon cinnamon **or** nutmeg, **or** both if desired

You may prefer to sweeten the taste of this luscious treat with extra cinnamon.

Makes 4 servings

In a large saucepan, simmer all the ingredients for at least 20 minutes, stirring occasionally. When the rice has cooked to a mushy consistency and much of the liquid has been absorbed, remove the saucepan from the heat and let the pudding cool a little. Pour into a large bowl, cover with plastic wrap, and keep in the fridge until chilled.

Scoop into individual dessert bowls and serve.

Note: This can be made gluten-free by using water *or* a nongluten liquid in place of the oat milk.

Nutty Brown Rice Pudding

This dessert features the rich taste of brown rice, especially when garnished with an extra dash of nutmeg.

Makes 4 servings

In a medium saucepan, combine all ingredients and bring to a boil, then reduce the heat and simmer for at least 30 minutes, until most of the liquid has been absorbed and the rice is almost mushy.

Remove the saucepan from the heat and let the pudding cool a little. Pour into a bowl, cover with plastic wrap, and chill in the fridge.

Scoop into individual dessert bowls and serve.

Note: This can be made gluten-free by using water *or* a nongluten liquid in place of the oat milk.

1½ cups oat milk

2 cups cooked whole grain brown rice

⅓ cup maple syrup *or* honey

½ cup raisins (optional)

1 teaspoon cinnamon *or* nutmeg, *or* both

Gluten-Free Almost Chocolate Pudding

2 medium avocados, pitted and peeled

1 tablespoon vanilla extract, alcohol-free

½ teaspoon sea salt

½ cup organic cocoa powder *or* ¾ cup carob powder

¼ cup agave nectar

¼ cup yacon syrup

The secret ingredient in this will amaze you! Imagine, the creamy goodness of avocados in a dessert pudding.

Makes approximately 2 servings.

Place all ingredients into the bowl of a food processor. Process until combined and smooth. Spoon into a container and refrigerate until well chilled.

Serve in individual dessert bowls.

Variation: This also makes a great chocolate pie—just double the recipe, spoon into the baked Dough Crust (see page 70), and refrigerate to set.

Note: If you're feeling adventurous and can't tolerate chocolate, try Raw Organic Cacao Powder which has a light, delightful flavor and is rich in antioxidants and minerals.

Fruit Sherbet

Refreshing sherbets are often overlooked because they are made with fruit rather than heavy cream. Be sure to serve in chilled dishes; sherbet melts quicker than ice cream.

Makes 4 servings

1 tablespoon unflavored gelatin

¼ cup cold water

2 cups fruit juice, any type except pineapple

1 cup chopped fruit, any type except pineapple

In a freezer-safe nonmetal mixing bowl, dissolve the gelatin in the cold water, stirring to dissolve it completely. Add the fruit juice and chopped fruit. Place the bowl in the freezer and leave it until the mixture is "mushy" ice, testing every 20 minutes or so.

Once the mixture has become mushy, remove the bowl from the freezer and beat the sherbet until fluffy. Return the bowl to the freezer and freeze until solid, usually overnight.

Scoop into individual dessert bowls and serve.

Raspberry Sorbet

1¾ cups water

1¾ cups sugar *or* equivalent sweetener

3 tablespoons lemon juice

½ tablespoon crème de cassis (black currant liqueur)

3 pints raspberries, rinsed

This has an intense, delightful raspberry flavor, brightened up by the lemon juice.

Makes 4 servings

In a medium saucepan, combine the water and sugar *or* equivalent sweetener. Bring to a boil to dissolve sugar *or* equivalent sweetener completely, stirring frequently. Boil for an additional 2 minutes. Remove the saucepan from the heat and stir in the lemon juice and crème de cassis. Pour the sorbet mixture into a large bowl and let it cool completely.

In a blender or food processor, puree the raspberries and strain them through a fine wire mesh strainer to remove all the seeds, then pour the pureed raspberries into the cooled sorbet mixture and stir thoroughly. Refrigerate until completely chilled (several hours).

Pour the chilled sorbet into a shallow baking pan or several ice cube trays and freeze until almost solid. Break the sorbet into chunks (or remove cubes from trays) and puree again in a blender or food processor.

Pour the sorbet into a freezer-safe bowl or container and freeze it for at least 1 hour before serving. Sorbet should be fairly solid, but not completely frozen. Spoon into individual dessert bowls and serve.

*My Kid's **Allergic to Everything** Dessert Cookbook*

Shortbread

This shortbread works very well for strawberry shortcake when you use brown or date sugar, but it can also be made with granulated sugar and different, lighter flours, like rice and barley, for a dessert-type cookie.

Makes one 8-inch square dessert *or* one 9-inch round dessert

Preheat oven to 300°F. Use one ungreased 8-inch cake pan *or* one ungreased 9-inch springform pan.

Cream together the margarine *or* oil, sugar *or* equivalent sweetener, and vanilla very well. Slowly blend in the flour, ½ cup at a time, mixing well after each addition. Press the dough evenly into the baking pan; then, using the back of a fork, press the tines around the edges of the dough to make a scored pattern, and press the points of the tines all over the surface of the dough to make a dotted pattern.

Bake for 45 to 50 minutes or until the center is almost firm to the touch and the surface has become light golden color.

Remove the shortbread from the oven and, leaving it in the baking pan, slice it immediately into wedges or squares. Cool and serve.

1 cup softened margarine *or* mild tasting oil

¼ cup sugar *or* equivalent sweetener

½ teaspoon vanilla extract, alcohol-free

2 cups flour (e.g., 1 cup oat, ½ cup barley, and ½ cup millet; *or* see chart, page 10–13)

Tapioca Pudding

2 cups water *or* any type fruit juice

3 tablespoons pearled tapioca, any size

1 teaspoon vanilla extract, alcohol-free

This wonderful recipe is very good, and simple to make.

Makes 2 to 4 servings

In a large saucepan, bring the water *or* juice to a boil. Stir in the tapioca pearls and let the mixture come to a boil again, then immediately remove the saucepan from the heat. Cover the saucepan and let the tapioca sit for 3 minutes. Return the saucepan to the stove, remove the cover, and bring the tapioca to a boil again, allowing the mixture to boil for 5 minutes, stirring two or three times a minute. Remove the saucepan from the heat and stir in the vanilla.

Pour the tapioca into a serving bowl and chill it in the refrigerator before serving.

Breakfast Ideas

10

Are you used to grabbing the variety cereal boxes at the store? Has breakfast always meant frying up some eggs and bacon or tossing sliced bread into the toaster and grabbing the butter and grape jelly? Get ready for some new ideas! Even grownups will enjoy these breakfast treats: some familiar old favorites, like pancakes and muffins, some new mouth-awakening flavors, like granola and apricot jam. Use these recipes as the groundwork for setting a whole new breakfast table, changing and adding ideas and ingredients of your own as you go along.

Pancakes and waffles are a wonderful and filling breakfast. Pancakes are ready to be turned over in the frying pan when a shine starts to disappear from the top of the batter and tiny bubbles appear around the edges. Flip them over and cook for about half the amount of time on the other side. You will get a feel for when they have cooked all the way through after you've made a few.

For homemade jams, jellies, and preserves, test for doneness by dripping a small amount of the jam or jelly, while it is simmering, onto a spoon and placing the spoon in the freezer for five minutes. (Keep the jam or jelly simmering.) Then touch and taste the sample on the spoon. It should be thick but not hard, and just sweet enough. If it seems thin or runny, cook or microwave the jam for another five minutes, then retest.

Buckwheat Pancakes or Waffles

1 cup oatmeal

1½ cups buckwheat flour

¼ teaspoon salt (optional)

1 teaspoon baking powder

¼ cup water *or* soy milk *or* rice milk *or* almond milk

1 tablespoon allowable margarine *or* mild tasting oil

1 teaspoon honey

Pancakes just taste better made from scratch. The oatmeal and buckwheat flour makes a tasty combination.

Makes 8 to 10 medium pancakes, 18 to 20 silver dollar pancakes, or 2 to 4 large waffles

Place the oatmeal in a blender or food processor and mix on high until ground into a coarse flour.

In a medium bowl, mix all ingredients until well blended and almost all the lumps are gone. Let the batter sit for several minutes to thicken; then stir vigorously by hand for several minutes more.

Pour the desired amount of batter for each pancake or waffle into a preheated oiled frying pan or waffle iron. Cook until bubbles appear around the edges of each pancake. Flip the pancake over and cook for about half of the time on the other side. For waffles, check the instructions for your waffle maker and cook for the recommended time. Serve hot.

Mary's Wheat-Free Pancake and Waffle Mix

This easy-to-store mix is very lightly spiced, aromatic when cooking, and much less expensive than ready-to-use wheat-free mixes.

Makes 30 to 36 medium pancakes, 60 silver dollar pancakes, or 9 to 12 large waffles

1 cup oat flour

1 cup buckwheat flour

1 cup spelt flour

¼ teaspoon cinnamon

¼ teaspoon nutmeg

¼ teaspoon allspice

3 teaspoons baking powder

5 teaspoons Ener-G Egg Replacer powder

Combine all ingredients well. This mix can be stored in an airtight jar or container in the fridge for up to four months.

To make 10 medium pancakes, 20 silver dollar pancakes, or 3 to 4 large waffles: In a medium bowl beat 1 cup of mix with ¾ cup any liquid (water, soy milk, rice milk, oat milk, *or* almond milk). Drop the batter onto a lightly oiled preheated frying pan over medium heat. When the pancake batter becomes dull on top and the edges begin to show air bubbles, approximately 3 to 4 minutes, flip the pancakes over and cook for approximately 2 minutes on the other side. For waffles, check the instructions for your waffle maker and cook for the recommended time.

Note: You can also make a huge batch of pancakes or waffles and store them, two to a ziplock bag, in the freezer. They heat up nicely in the toaster.

Wilma's Gluten-Free Coconut Pancakes

These delicious pancakes have a mild flavor and a light fluffy texture.

Makes approximately 4 medium pancakes

6 teaspoons Ener-G Egg Replacer powder, whipped with 6 tablespoons water to a firm foam

2 tablespoons tahini, creamy with no lumps

1 tablespoon coconut oil, warmed (for mix)

3 tablespoons hemp milk *or* any allowable milk

3 teaspoons agave powder sweetener

¼ teaspoon sea salt

4 tablespoons coconut flour

½ teaspoon baking powder

1 tablespoon coconut oil (for frying pan)

In a large bowl, mix together Ener-G Egg Replacer mixture, tahini, coconut oil, hemp milk, agave powder sweetener, and sea salt. Add the baking powder and coconut flour and stir until thoroughly mixed.

Heat 1 tablespoon coconut oil in a skillet on a medium flame. As you make more pancakes, add more coconut oil if the pancakes start to stick.

Spoon approximately 2 tablespoonfuls of batter onto the skillet, making pancakes about 3 inches in diameter. Swirl the spoon over the top of each pancake, making sure that the batter is between ¼ to ½ inch thick. This will assure that the pancakes cook thoroughly and do not have a doughy or undercooked texture. After two minutes, check the pancake undersides; if browning nicely, flip over and cook for another minute or two.

Serve with fruit puree *or* maple syrup *or* one of our delectable jams!

My Kid's Allergic to Everything Dessert Cookbook

Muffalicious Muffins

This basic recipe, and all its variations, are totally delicious!

Makes 12 large or 24 regular muffins

Preheat oven to 400°F. Line large 6-cup cupcake tins *or* 12-cup cupcake tins with cupcake papers.

Combine the oat bran *or* flours, brown sugar *or* equivalent sweetener, baking powder, salt, and Ener-G Egg Replacer powder well. Add the milk, honey, and margarine *or* oil and mix well. Add the cranberries and banana, mixing only until the fruits are blended into the batter. If the batter feels too stiff, add a little more milk *or* some fruit juice by teaspoonfuls until the desired consistency is reached.

Fill the cupcake papers two-thirds full.

Bake for 15 minutes or until muffin tops are lightly browned and an inserted toothpick comes out clean.

May be served warm, or stored in the refrigerator or freezer and microwaved on high for 30 seconds to reheat.

Variations: In place of the cranberries and bananas, try the following:

½ cup finely chopped apple with 1 teaspoon grated ginger, cinnamon, or allspice

1 cup cherries or blueberries

½ cup crushed pineapple with ½ teaspoon grated orange peel

½ cup finely chopped allowable nuts or seeds

With any of the above, add our streusel topping (see page 71)

2 cups oat bran *or* any combination of sticky flours (see page 7)

¼ cup brown sugar, packed, *or* equivalent sweetener

2 teaspoons baking powder

½ teaspoon salt

3 teaspoons Ener-G Egg Replacer powder

1 cup soy milk *or* goat's milk *or* almond milk *or* oat milk

¼ cup honey

2 tablespoons allowable margarine *or* mild tasting oil

½ to 1 cup cranberries, fresh *or* frozen (to taste)

1 small banana, mashed

Buckwheat Muffins

¾ cup buckwheat flour

¾ cup any other flour (e.g. ¼ cup soy *or* rice and ½ cup millet *or* oat)

2 teaspoons baking powder

½ teaspoon salt

1 cup water *or* soy milk *or* rice milk

5 tablespoons honey

¼ cup mild tasting oil

2 egg yolks *or* 3 teaspoons Ener-G Egg Replacer powder mixed with 2 teaspoons water

1 teaspoon vanilla extract, alcohol-free

½ cup raisins (optional)

½ cup sunflower seeds (optional)

These wholesome breakfast muffins can be enjoyed any time of the day.

Makes 10 large *or* 15 regular muffins

Preheat oven to 350°F. Line large 6-cup cupcake tins *or* 12-cup cupcake tins with cupcake papers.

In a large bowl, mix together the flours, baking powder, and salt. Add the water *or* milk, honey, oil, egg yolks *or* Ener-G Egg Replacer powder mixture, and vanilla; beat until smooth. Add raisins and seeds, if desired, and mix until well blended.

Fill the cupcake papers two-thirds full.

Bake for 20 minutes or until tops of muffins are lightly browned and an inserted toothpick comes out clean.

My Kid's *Allergic to Everything* Dessert Cookbook

Sweet Granola

This recipe has been modified to use flax oil, which contains an essential fatty acid shown to be helpful with skin problems and middle ear infections. However, any mild tasting oil or margarine can be used and the results are always delicious!

Makes approximately 7 cups

Preheat oven to 300°F. Use one ungreased cookie sheet or large shallow baking pan.

In a large bowl, mix the oil *or* allowable shortening *or* margarine with the honey *or* maple syrup, brown sugar *or* date sugar, and vanilla. Add the rolled oats, nuts, seeds, dates, and raisins; mix well. Spread the granola evenly onto the cookie sheet or baking pan and bake for 20 minutes. Remove the granola from the oven and turn it over completely; then bake for another 10 minutes. Remove the granola from the oven and stir well. Let it cool completely before storing.

The granola will keep well in a large jar in the cupboard or a covered bowl in the refrigerator for several weeks.

½ cup flax oil *or* any mild tasting oil *or* melted allowable shortening *or* melted margarine

½ cup honey *or* maple syrup

½ cup brown sugar, packed *or* date sugar

1 teaspoon vanilla extract, alcohol-free

4 cups rolled oats (regular, instant, *or* "quick")

1 cup cashews *or* almonds, slivered, sliced, or pieces (but not crushed)

½ cup flax seeds *or* sunflower seeds (optional)

1 cup chopped, pitted dates

1 cup raisins

Apricot Spread

8 ounces dried apricots

¾ cup water

¼ cup honey

1 tablespoon orange juice

¼ teaspoon cinnamon

This topping for can be used for wheat-free toast or as a filling for cookies. It is lower in sugar than jam.

Makes approximately 16 ounces

In a large saucepan, heat the apricots and water over a high heat until boiling. Reduce the heat and simmer for 15 minutes or until the apricots are very tender. Remove the saucepan from the heat, let sit for about 10 minutes, and then pour off the excess water. Stir in the honey, orange juice, and cinnamon.

Pour the mixture into a blender or food processor and blend until almost smooth.

Spoon the spread into two small (6- or 8-ounce) jars and store in the refrigerator. The apricot spread will keep for up to two months.

Orange & Honey Syrup

¾ cup honey

1 teaspoon allowable shortening *or* margarine

1 tablespoon orange zest

¼ cup orange juice

1 teaspoon orange extract, alcohol-free

We first tasted this syrup on waffles at a cozy bed-and-breakfast. It's a luxurious treat to be able to make this at home.

Makes approximately 1 cup

In a medium saucepan, heat the honey and allowable shortening *or* margarine over a medium heat until bubbling. Remove the saucepan from the heat and stir in the orange zest, juice, and extract, mixing well. Pour the syrup into a 10- or 12- ounce jar, cover and refrigerate. May be reheated if desired.

My Kid's *Allergic to Everything* Dessert Cookbook

Microwave Apricot Jam

This recipe is easy to vary for different lovely flavors. Dried apples or peaches may be used instead of apricots, and apple juice may be used instead of orange juice, for example.

Makes approximately 40 ounces

In a large microwave-safe bowl, combine the apricots, orange juice, and sugar *or* equivalent sweetener. Cover and microwave on high for 12 minutes.

Carefully remove the bowl and pour the mixture into a blender or food processor. Add the cinnamon, ginger, and lemon juice; blend until smooth.

Pour the jam into three 16-ounce jars, cover, and refrigerate. The jam will keep for several months.

16 ounces dried apricots

2½ cups orange juice

¾ cup sugar *or* equivalent sweetener

½ teaspoon cinnamon

¼ teaspoon ground dried ginger

1 tablespoon lemon juice

Easy Cherry Preserves

With the taste of sweet dark cherries, this is unbelievably good and sure to become a family favorite.

Makes approximately 40 ounces

In a large microwave-safe bowl, combine the cherries and the sugar *or* equivalent sweetener. Cover loosely and microwave on high for 12 minutes. Carefully remove the bowl and stir the cherry mixture to completely dissolve the sugar *or* sweetener; leave uncovered and microwave on high for another 40 to 45 minutes.

Carefully remove the bowl and pour the mixture into a blender or food processor, add the lemon juice, and blend until the cherries are coarsely pureed.

Pour into three 16-ounce jars, put on the lids, and refrigerate. The preserves will keep for several months.

36 ounces fresh *or* frozen dark cherries, pitted

½ cup sugar *or* equivalent sweetener

½ tablespoon lemon juice

Fresh Fast Peach Jam

1½ cups peaches, pitted, peeled, and chopped (2 medium peaches)

4 tablespoons sugar *or* equivalent sweetener

1 tablespoon arrowroot flour

¼ teaspoon ground dried ginger

¼ teaspoon ground allspice

1 teaspoon lemon juice

Capture the delicious sweet flavor of fresh peaches by making jam during the summer peach season.

Makes approximately 8 ounces

In a 1½-quart microwave safe bowl, combine all ingredients except the lemon juice. Microwave, uncovered, on high for 4 minutes. Stir the jam well, then microwave, uncovered, for an additional 3 to 4 minutes or until the jam begins to thicken.

Remove the bowl and, using a fork, mash any large chunks of peaches. Stir in the lemon juice and set the jam aside to cool until it is lukewarm.

Once it is cooled, spoon the jam into a 10-ounce jar and refrigerate overnight before using. The jam will keep for up to one month stored in the refrigerator.

Monumental Strawberry Jam

3 pints fresh strawberries, washed, hulled, and halved

1½ cups sugar *or* equivalent sweetener

1 tablespoon lemon juice

This jam has always been a favorite with our kids, and with their friends, too!

Makes approximately 32 ounces

In a large microwave-safe bowl, combine the strawberries, sugar *or* equivalent sweetener, and lemon juice. Cover loosely and microwave on high for 15 minutes. Stir the jam to completely dissolve the sugar *or* sweetener. Use a fork to mash down the strawberries. Leave uncovered and microwave for another 45 to 50 minutes.

Spoon the jam into two 16-ounce jars and refrigerate overnight before using. The jam will keep for up to several months stored in the refrigerator.

Smoothies

A smoothie is basically pitted or seeded fruit or fruit juice blended with ice, water, an allowable milk, or yogurt to make a very refreshing and low-calorie drink. It's a wonderful breakfast for kids during the hot summer months, and a quick one for schoolkids on those "oops, we're running late" days. Four basic recipes follow; try them and then try out your own variations.

One thing I've been doing lately is purchasing fresh seasonal organic fruits, washing and pitting or seeding them, and storing them in 8-ounce ziplock bags in the freezer for a winter smoothie treat.

Another trick I discovered is to put containers of soy milk, sheep's milk, or goat's milk yogurt in the freezer, then use them, instead of ice, with the fruit and liquid for a thicker, richer smoothie. The frozen yogurt will pop right out of the container.

Finally, a delicious option is to freeze fruit juices in the ice cube trays—use them instead of plain ice!

Berry Smoothie

1 ripe banana, chilled and peeled

½ cup strawberries, cleaned, hulled, and chilled

¼ cup pitted dates

1 tablespoon bee pollen (optional)

3 tablespoons honey

½ cup crushed ice *or* 3 small ice cubes

1 cup cold fruit juice (any type)

This berry smoothie tastes great and contains antioxidants, vitamins, and other nutrients. Try it as a great healthy after-school snack.

Makes 1 serving

In a blender, puree the banana, strawberries, and dates until smooth. Add the bee pollen, if using, and honey, blending until smooth. Add the fruit juice and ice and blend on high speed until smooth.

Serve immediately.

Fruit Smoothie

1 very ripe cantaloupe, peeled, seeded, and diced

2 tablespoons frozen orange, lemonade, *or* limeade concentrate, undiluted

1 tablespoon honey

¼ teaspoon cinnamon

¼ teaspoon cardamom

1 liter unflavored seltzer water

This is a refreshing and frothy drink for a hot summer day.

Makes approximately 6 servings

In a blender, puree the cantaloupe until smooth. Add the frozen juice, honey, cinnamon, and cardamom; blend until smooth. Chill for several hours.

To serve, stir equal amounts of the smoothie with the seltzer water until well mixed.

Power Smoothie

A delicious and satisfying pick-me-up for breakfast.

Makes 1 serving

In a blender, mix the oat bran flakes on high speed until almost powdered. Add the cold water and let sit for several minutes. Add the yogurt, berries, and lemon peel and blend on high speed until smooth.

Serve immediately.

¼ cup oat bran flakes*

⅓ cup cold water

1 container of allowable lemon yogurt

1 cup fresh *or* frozen berries (any kind)

½ teaspoon grated lemon peel

*Note: Arrowhead Mills makes corn-free and vanilla-free oat bran flakes. Health Valley has a variety that contains corn flour and vanilla flavor.

Tropical Smoothie

This smoothie recipe with a kick of ginger is great for the hot summer months and will transport you to an island getaway in your own backyard!

Makes 1 serving

Place all ingredients in a blender and mix on high speed until well blended.

Serve immediately.

¼ cup cold orange juice

¼ cup cold pineapple juice

1 tablespoon coconut milk

½ banana, peeled, *or* ½ mango, peeled and sliced

¼ teaspoon fresh, peeled, grated ginger root

½ cup crushed ice *or* 3 small ice cubes

Way Cool Smoothie

4 allowable yogurts, in 6-ounce *or* 8-ounce cups

24 ounces of fresh fruit, divided into 4 portions, 6-ounces each

Fruit juice, any type

This is delicious and icy cold!

Makes 1 serving

Place the yogurt cups in the freezer. Put the freezer bags of fresh fruit in the freezer, 6 ounces to a bag.

When your family is ready for cool smoothies on a hot day, put the contents of 1 frozen yogurt cup and 1 frozen fruit bag in the blender. Add 1 cup of fruit juice (such as orange) and blend until smooth. Serve immediately.

Emerald Blossom Breakfast

1 cup seedless green grapes, partially frozen

1 cup raw chard *or* spinach *or* lettuce leaves, washed and stems removed

1 banana, peeled, cut into pieces, and partially frozen

1 raw apple, peeled, cored, and cut into 8 chunks

1 teaspoon cinnamon

1 cup water

Try experimenting with your own combinations of the fruits and vegetables your family likes the most.

Makes 1 serving

Combine all ingredients in blender. Blend on high until smooth and creamy. If the fruit is not frozen, add 4 to 6 ice cubes and blend on high until the ice cubes are broken down. This will make the smoothie cold and thick. Serve immediately.

Variation: Add 1 cup partially frozen strawberries or 1 cup partially frozen blueberries instead of the apple.

Mango Breakfast Delight

You can hide any mild leafy green vegetable—such as spinach, dandelion leaves, or spring garden mix—in this nutritious smoothie.

Makes 2 servings

Combine all ingredients in blender. Blend on high until smooth and creamy. Add more water to get the texture that you and your family enjoy. Serve immediately.

1 mango, peeled, pitted, and cut into 1-inch chunks

½ head romaine lettuce, washed and torn into pieces (discard stem)

1 plum, pitted and cut into 1-inch chunks

¼ avocado, pitted and peeled

2 cups water

6 ice cubes

Can I Still Shop at My Local Supermarket?

11

This chapter does not endorse any products, nor does it contain a complete list of all available food products. It merely lists foods we now commonly purchase that are readily available at most local grocery stores, along with ingredient information we have discovered by trial and error.

Your child may have an allergy to a food that is not fully addressed in this book, such as gluten. You may use the list of gluten flours in chapter 1 to help you eliminate gluten products from your child's diet. There are also many other good sources for help in creating gluten-free meals (see chapter 13).

For any allergy you are coping with, your first source of information is your eyes: be sure to read all ingredients lists carefully. Many ingredients are commonly known in the food industry under several names. Ask your doctor for help with other possible names for the ingredients your child is allergic to. Call a manufacturer's toll-free phone number or go to their Web site and request specific information about labeling and ingredients sources, additives, and packaging.

Also, be aware that many cardboard containers, even those made from post-consumer recycled materials, may be made from or include ground-up cornhusk and corncob but components for packaging materials are not required to be listed—call and ask.

Finally, remember that many children's medicines have corn-based sweeteners added to make them more palatable; the colored sweetener the pharmacist can add for an additional cost is corn-based; and many children's vitamins have a corn-based sweetener and/or cornstarch added for taste and stability. Ask your doctor to verify the ingredients in any medication, and ask your pharmacist for specific labeling information on medicines, additions, and vitamins.

The following list, which is not all-inclusive, gives common and brand names for these foods, or their by-products:

EGG

Some labels list albumin, and watch for anything starting with "ovo-".

WHEAT

Beware of anything listing Accent, bran, bread crumbs, bulgur or burghol, couscous, cracker meal, durum, farina, many forms of "filler," gluten, graham, HVP (hydrolyzed vegetable protein), many types of modified food starch, MSG, orzo, Postum, pumpernickel, seitan, semolina, tabbouleh, some varieties of tempeh, wheat germ, and some forms of yeast.

BAKING POWDER

Most commercial baking powders have cornstarch added to insure a free-pouring lump-free product. Plain baking soda is sometimes an allowable alternative (see page 29), and cornstarch-free baking powders (also called cereal-free), such as Featherweight, Whole Foods' 365 generic brand, or Hain, are available at most health food stores.

CANNED FOODS

We have discovered a concern about the chemical Bisphenol A (BPA), which has been used for years in clear plastic bottles and food can liners. *Consumer Reports* magazine tested 19 name-brand foods, both organic and nonorganic, and found BPA in almost all of them. The Food and Drug Administration has yet to decide what a safe level of exposure to BPA will be, which some studies have linked to reproductive abnormalities and a heightened risk of breast cancer, prostate cancer, diabetes, and heart disease. Whenever possible, we buy fresh or frozen fruits and vegetables.

CATSUP

The only commercial brand we found which was free of corn-syrup sweetener was a kosher catsup carried during Passover. All other catsups had corn syrup sweeteners, and many also had artificial ingredients with which we were not comfortable.

CEREALS, BREAKFAST

Plain oatmeals (long-cooking and quick), most unflavored instant oatmeals, Rice Chex, and puffed rice cereals are all corn- and wheat-free.

CHOCOLATE CANDY

Many confectioners' boxed chocolates, such as Fannie May or Fannie Farmer, have an egg-white gloss brushed onto the candies for consumer eye appeal. Plain chocolate bars, such as Hershey's, do not have the egg-white gloss, but remember that milk chocolate bars use a cow's milk derivative and their ingredients must be checked carefully. Also, "white" chocolate is derived from the cocoa bean, therefore its use should be verified by your doctor if your child has a chocolate allergy.

COCOA

Cocoa powder and chocolate powder usually have cornstarch added to insure a dry, lump-free and free-flowing product; if specific ingredient information is not available on the label, play it safe and melt baker's chocolate for your baking needs. Carob powder and carob chips are wonderful chocolatey alternatives if you are dealing with a chocolate allergy, but you must check their labels for corn and cow's milk additives. Both chocolate chips and carob chips usually have those additives because they ensure a reasonable melting point while allowing the chip to retain its shape.

CONFECTIONERS' SUGAR or POWDERED SUGAR

Most confectioners' or powdered sugars have cornstarch added to insure a dry and free-flowing product. You can make a reasonable substitute by slowly pouring small amounts of granulated sugar into your food processor or blender while it is on a high speed (see page 22). This will not give you as fine a powder but still works well.

COOKIES

Almost all cookies use wheat flour and some sort of corn sweetener, a lot use butter or some form of cow's milk products, and a few use eggs or egg products. In addition to health food stores, many supermarkets now carry gluten-free and allergen-free cookies, but not in abundance. There are also several Web sites that sell allergen-free cookies and other desserts. Please check labels for ingredients appropriate to your child.

CORN

Check the labels for bran, caramel, cereal, cerelose, dextrose, fructose, germ meal, glucose, gluten meal, grits, hominy, HVP (hydrolyzed vegetable protein), Karo, maize, maltodextrin, masa harina, modified food starch, polenta, pozole, sucrose, and xanthan gum.

COW'S MILK

Look for anything containing casein, curd, lactalbumin, lactoglobulin, lactose, rennet, sodium caseinate, whey. (Note: calcium carbonate and calcium lactate are not dairy-derived ingredients.)

CRACKERS

Rice crackers now come in lots of different flavors. These are healthy and crunchy alternatives to potato chips, popcorn, and other snacks popular with kids. Several varieties of Ry Krisp are also wheat- and corn-free, and many supermarkets and restaurants have these available.

FRUIT ROLL-UPS or FRUIT LEATHERS

Some commercial fruit roll-ups do not contain corn syrup sweeteners. You may object, however, to the amounts of artificial coloring and flavoring they use. Further, we are concerned about sulfites and nitrates used in the drying process--some studies have linked nitrates to different types of cancers. A fun family alternative is to use a dehydrator and make your own.

GELATINS

Several brands of boxed flavored gelatin mixes are corn-free; however, many use artificial sweeteners and we are concerned about their alleged detrimental impact on brain cells.

ICE CREAM

Some ice creams, such as Breyer's Chocolate and Breyer's Mint Chocolate Chip, do not contain eggs, egg whites, or corn syrup sweeteners. However, all ice creams, ice milks, gelatos, sherbets, many sorbets, and frozen yogurts are made with cow's milk. Most health food stores and many local supermarkets now carry frozen tofu desserts, which are delightful alternatives. Many health food stores also have frozen rice milk, coconut milk, and hemp milk "ice creams" that are delicious.

JUICES

Many brands of frozen and fresh fruit juices are made from juice and water only, but check labels carefully for any corn-based sweeteners. At restaurants, an assurance that orange or grapefruit juice is freshly squeezed should be sufficient.

MALT

Most malts are derived from barley and are allowable as nonallergenic products. Malt also provides additional minerals and vitamins when mixed with alternative milks, such as rice milk or soy milk.

MARGARINE

We found only two brands of margarines in our local supermarket that were corn- and dairy-free: Parkay Squeeze Spread in a plastic bottle and a generic store brand of spread in a large plastic tub at Jewel Food Stores. Your supermarket may offer its own generic brand, but be sure to check the label for allowable vegetable-based ingredients. Since most people with an allergy to cow's milk are reacting either to the whey or to the casein, check with your allergist to find out if either is allowable in your child's diet. There are also goat butters available from Cabrima and Meyenberg, if your child's allergy is strictly limited to cow's milk products. Earth Balance makes a vegan "natural shortening," but we have not tried this product. Note: any product with the symbol (P) or the word "Pareve" or "Parve" is guaranteed to be dairy-free. Pareve or Parve, noted with the (P) symbol, means the product conforms to Jewish kosher dietary restrictions and is therefore cow's milk free.

MAYONNAISE

All contain egg; some also contain corn oil. Use an egg-free, corn-oil-free salad dressing instead, such as Vegenaise by Follow Your Heart.

MILK

We have found soy milk and goat's milk readily available at our local supermarkets. Rice milk is also becoming more readily available, especially in the Hispanic foods aisle. Tofu drinks, oat, hemp, almond milks, and powdered goat's milk can be found at health food stores.

MOLASSES

Commercial brands of light and dark molasses, which are used in many baked goods such as gingersnap cookies, are allowable and do not contain corn products. However, it is a by-product of cane sugar processing.

MUSTARD

Many contain wheat flour as a thickener; find a brand that clearly states all its ingredients.

OILS

Many oils at your supermarket are clearly labeled and contain only one type of pure oil, such as canola or olive. However, carefully check bottles marked "vegetable oil" as they may contain corn oil.

POTATO CHIPS

Some brands of potato chips are deep-fried in oils other than corn oil. A rigorous label search may reward you. Caution: labels reading "all vegetable oil" may mean corn oil or peanut oil is used with other oils. If the list of ingredients is not specific and your store manager or the manufacturer cannot supply the information, play it safe and avoid that product. If your family absolutely demands chips, investigate one of the several baked chips available.

PUDDINGS

Several brands of ready-to-eat pudding cups are wheat- and egg-free, but not corn- and dairy-free. For example, Del Monte uses corn and tapioca as the bases for their modified food starch, and beet sugar or cane sugar as the bases for their sweetener. However, remember that these products contain cow's milk.

RICE

Many brands of rice are "enriched": the nutritious hull has been stripped off, vitamins and minerals have been artificially added to the kernels, and the final product has been dusted with cornstarch to keep the grains loose and dry. And remember, the healthiest, most nutritious rice is brown rice.

SALT

Most brands of iodized table salt contain dextrose as a stabilizing ingredient, and many also contain sodium silicoaluminate, an aluminum by-product, which may concern you as it does us. However, many groceries also carry sea salt and "pickling" or "preserving" salts. These function just as well as iodized table salt for cooking or baking, and are dextrose- and sodium silicoaluminate-free. Some manufacturers offer iodine-free table and cooking salts that do not contain dextrose. If you are concerned about a lack of iodine in your child's diet and the resultant possible impact on their thyroid, discuss this with your doctor or licensed nutritionist. Other good sources of iodine include shellfish, saltwater fish, dried seaweed, cod liver oil, and vegetables grown very near an ocean. Also, please remember that kosher "sour salt" is not an allowable substitute for table salt or for baking desserts.

SHORTENING

Most brands of shortening contain corn products and other allergens. There are, however, several brands available, such as Earth Balance, which are vegan and corn-free.

SODA POP

Soda almost always has a corn syrup sweetener. Diet soda uses artificial sweeteners. Some supermarkets and many health food stores carry natural sodas in many different flavors. Or you can make your own: use an allowable fruit juice concentrate and add a spoonful or two, to taste, to a clear seltzer water.

SORGHUM

A sweetener derived from the domestic grain, sorghum is allowable and does not contain corn products. However, it has a very strong taste that some people don't like.

SOY SAUCE

Most brands of soy sauce use wheat in the distillation process and may contain alcohol from an unknown source. Carefully check labels for an allowable soy or tamari sauce.

VANILLA

Many brands of vanilla extract, imitation vanilla flavoring, and other types of extracts and flavorings use grain alcohol as the base in the extraction process. That grain alcohol is usually wheat-based. Most also list "corn syrup sweetener" or "dextrose" as additional ingredients. If your local store does not carry an allowable vanilla such as Frontier or Cook's, a specialty or gourmet food store or health food store will usually have one, or you can order them online. You can also try making your own (see page 36).

VINEGAR

White (clear) vinegars are distilled from a variety of grains, fruits, and vegetables; cider (brown) vinegar normally uses apple cider as its base. Since cider vinegar usually has as high a level of acidity (the important factor in baking, cooking, and pickling) as white vinegar, people with grain and potato allergies may use cider vinegar with confidence.

YOGURT

Yogurt is almost always a cow's milk product. Most health food stores now carry a creamy yogurt-like tofu or soy product, a goat's milk yogurt, and a coconut milk yogurt. These are tasty alternatives, and are available flavored.

If this list has you quaking at the thought of spending the next three days reading supermarket labels just to be able to get dinner on the table, don't give up! It is time-consuming and frightening at first, but we promise it will get easier. And you will also receive the best reward possible—a healthy, happy child.

Finally, remember that fresh organic fruits and vegetables are a great snack!

Green Cleaning and Safe Pesticides

Keeping our homes clean is almost a full-time job in itself. Since you already spend time cleaning, and now are even more concerned because your child's allergies may include pollen, spores, and dust-mites, why not simply use "friendly" cleaning products and botanical, or plant-derived, pesticides instead of pouring more chemicals around? This chapter begins with cleaning tips, continues with gardening tips, and ends with a list of botanical suppliers and brochures for more detailed information. Insecticide and pesticide suppliers and your local nursery are usually more than happy to discuss your particular gardening or insect problem. Just be careful about using any chemical. A sales clerk's assurance that minimal use is fine doesn't *guarantee* its safety. The National Pesticide Information Center has a Web site (http://npic.orst.edu) and a free phone hotline (800-858-7378) that provide objective, science-based information so you can make informed decisions about pesticides. GreenPeace (www.greenpeace.org) has some lovely free literature and online information about ecologically safe cleaning supplies and alternatives to commercial products.

Suggested commercial products and manufacturers can be found in the Resources chapter (see page 169).

HOUSEHOLD CLEANERS

Baking Soda

A wonderful alternative to chlorine powders and liquids. Baking soda and vinegar can be used to "boil" out mineral deposits in glasses, pots, and pans; and to eliminate calcified areas on the tub and bathroom sink (with a little elbow grease). If you use boxed baking soda as a deodorant in the freezer or refrigerator, you can use the baking soda as a cleaning product once the recommended three months are up.

Dishwasher Detergent

A more chemical-free dishwasher detergent may be made by combining a powdered commercial detergent with equal amounts of powdered borax and washing soda (2 cups commercial detergent plus 2 cups borax plus 2 cups washing soda). Greenpeace (see page 167) recommends eliminating commercial detergents entirely, but I have found that a film similar to hard-water spots coats my dishes and glasses when I don't use any commercial detergent, so I cheat and add a little bit.

Flax Soap

A good alternative to commercial linoleum cleansers, although you will have to rinse carefully to get rid of the dull effect it may leave on no-wax floors. It is also wonderful for washing wood in your house, including floors, furniture, and kitchen cabinets. Most furniture made since World War I is sealed at the factory with long lasting, impenetrable lacquers, and the wood underneath does not need to be "nourished" by oils or waxes; it can be cleaned and treated well by using ¼ cup flax soap to one gallon of water, washed with a clean sponge or rag, and dried with a clean cloth.

Vinegar, White

A good alternative to commercial cleansers and ammonia when cleaning windows and leather desktops. It also works for dusting: combine 2 tablespoons white vinegar with 1 quart warm water, pour into a spray bottle, and spray onto a clean cloth for dusting and cleaning leather, or directly onto mirrors or windows for streak-free cleaning. Do not use if a corn allergy is present.

ARE YOU A GREEN CLEANING MACHINE?

Solid Waste Agency of Northern Cook County

You will be, after reading the Solid Waste Agency of Northern Cook County (SWANCC) Eco-Cleaning Guide, which provides less toxic or nontoxic substitutes to commercial products for the entire home and is packed full of eco-friendly tips along the way.

Reasons to Use Environmental Cleaning Products:
- Decrease exposure to ingredients that may be harmful to your health
- Provide cleaner air in your home environment
- Save money as you make your own cleaning products
- Reduce your use of nonrenewable resources and make smaller carbon footprints

Harmful chemicals are frequently used as ingredients in household products (e.g., paints, varnishes, moth repellents, aerosol sprays, cleaning supplies, disinfectants, cosmetics, and dry-cleaned clothing). One way to make sure you know what is in your cleaning products is to make them yourself. You might be surprised that many of the ingredients are already in your kitchen. Some of the most useful, natural cleaners include lemon, vinegar, and baking soda. Among others are borax, club soda, corn meal, hydrogen peroxide, olive oil, salt, and toothpaste.

The Eco-Cleaning Guide is one way to make a difference by using safer alternatives to commercial cleaning products. Explore the Eco-Cleaning Guide, available as a PDF file from their Web site.

SWANCC
2700 Patriot Boulevard
Suite 110
Glenview, IL 60026
847-724-9205
www.swancc.org/pdfs/Education/ecoCleaningGuide.pdf

Many thanks to Ms. Mary Allen, SWANCC Recycling and Education Director, and Ms. Elizabeth Grisham, P.A., for their assistance and labors of love in compiling this information.

INDOOR PEST CONTROL

ANTS

Powdered boric acid, a constituent of many naturally occuring minerals, is an effective ant control. Take a jar lid, spoon in a little jam, jelly, or honey, sprinkle generously with powdered boric acid, and leave it where you have noticed ants. They will climb in to eat the sweets, ingest the boric acid, and trail it home to the ant colony. Within a week the colony will be all or mostly all dead. Please keep boric acid away from carpets and furniture as it has a corrosive effect on these materials. Please also keep it away from children and pets: it is harmful in large enough doses. I recently found that my pharmacist removed the jars of powdered boric acid from the store shelves and I had to order it. Since the order required six jars or more, I went in with a few neighbors and we each got one, making a more pesticide-free neighborhood!

Tannic acid, an ingredient in caffeinated teas, is also a good insecticide. In a large nonaluminum pot, boil 1 gallon of water with 12 to 16 teabags, then let it steep until the water is almost black. Remove the teabags and pour the tea around the outside of your home, paying special attention to areas where you think ants have built their colonies. It may take several gallons over a week or two, but the ants will diminish or disappear. This must be redone each time it rains.

COCKROACHES

Many people have found that sprinkling powdered boric acid in cupboards and along baseboards helps to control cockroaches. Whole bay leaves placed in drawers and cupboards also seem to be a fairly effective control; fresh bay leaves work better and faster than dried bay leaves, but dried bay leaves will work eventually.

DUST MITES

These tiny insects live in carpeting, furniture, mattresses, pillows, stuffed animals—just about anything people can own. Vacuuming and mopping alone will not eliminate them. Allergy Control Products, Inc. (see page 172) sells a spray which kills dust mites and is nontoxic to people and animals.

FLEAS

Brewer's yeast and/or a garlic supplement added to your dog's or cat's food will help control fleas and is undetectable to the animals as they eat. For dogs, try using one scant tablespoon of brewer's yeast every other day, and/or one garlic tablet weekly, ground and mixed into your pet's food. You may have to increase the dosage if you see no effect in a week. For cats, try using one scant teaspoon of brewer's yeast every other day, and/or one small garlic tablet weekly. If you don't have garlic tablets, finely chop one small fresh garlic clove. A tiny amount of eucalyptus oil spread carefully on the dog's or cat's collar will also help control fleas, but don't use so much that it can seep into the pet's skin or rub off where they can lick it—even botanical solutions can be deadly to a small animal! If available, use eucalyptus leaves or lemon gum (*Eucalyptus citriodora*) to make a "pillow" for the pet's bed; it is not as effective as quickly, but certainly safer. Ecologically safe pyrethrin sprays, available at your local gardening center or by mail order (see page 168) can be used directly on animals (check the label or with your veterinarian for correct amounts). Please note that citrus solutions are toxic to pets, whether as a dip or as a wipe. Cedar chips and shavings, spread in the pet's pen or made into a pillow for the pet's bed, are definitely safe and do work—cedar is registered with the Environmental Protection Agency as a flea repellent. But please check with your veterinarian before using any form of insecticide.

HOUSEHOLD PLANT INSECTS AND MITES

A simple rinsing of the plant leaves in cool water in your sink every two to three weeks will eliminate most pests from your indoor plants. Scale insects are a more difficult problem: check with your state university's Cooperative Service Extension (see www.csrees.usda.gov/extension) or, if your community offers it, the Master Gardeners Program (see www.ahs.org/master_gardeners).

OUTDOOR PEST CONTROL

Always test the spray or powder on one or two leaves first, to determine a plant's sensitivity! If the leaves are OK after several days, you may use the spray or powder on the whole plant.

FUNGICIDES

Mix 1 teaspoon organic insecticidal soap like Safer's Soap, available at most commercial garden centers, nurseries, or online, with 3 to 4 teaspoons baking soda, 3 to 4 teaspoons vegetable oil, and 1 gallon tap water. Pour into spray bottles and spray all leaves on both sides several times for one week.

INSECT CONTROL

Sprays and Powders Safer's Soap is an effective pest control. Follow the container instructions for use.

Or, you can make your own outdoor garden pest control liquid by using one of the following recipes:

1. Mix 1 tablespoon dishwashing liquid, nitrate-, phosphate-, and corn-free, with 1 cup vegetable oil; add 1 or 2 teaspoons of this mixture to 1 cup tap water, pour into a spray bottle, and spray your plant leaves and fruits.

2. Put 3 to 4 garlic cloves in the blender with 1 cup tap water. Blend until liquefied, then pour the mixture into a spray bottle, and spray your plant leaves and fruits.

3. Make your own pyrethrum spray by purchasing pyrethrum concentrate from your local nursery and following the directions on the container; or grow and pluck *Chrysanthemum cinerariifolium* flower heads when two or three outer rows of petals have opened in the central yellow discs. Dry the flower heads either in sunlight or in your oven set on the lowest temperature, then grind the heads into a powder using a coffee mill, blender, or mortar and pestle (clean the coffee mill thoroughly afterwards). Pour 10 grams of the powder into a dark-colored bottle (light will weaken the solution) and add 4 ounces of denatured alcohol; shake and let stand for 24 hours at room temperature. Pour into a spray bottle and spray directly onto affected plants. Pyrethrum kills insects and fish on contact, but is considered safe in very small amounts when it comes into surface contact

with humans and warm-blooded animals.

4. Diatomaceous earth (a finely ground powder made from the fossilized remains of primitive plants known as diatoms) sprinkled in your garden area will kill exoskeletar (chitinous, or with the skeleton on the outside) insects. The sharp edges of these microscopically small ground plants pierce the insect's shell, allowing its vital fluids to leak out. Please be careful when spreading diatomaceous earth, because it should not be inhaled; use a mask and scatter carefully when there is no wind.

All these mixtures break down after exposure to sunlight and moisture and will rinse off with rain and dew. They are not recommended for indoor plant use. You must be careful using any type of pest control, indoors or outside.

Beneficial Insects Beneficial insects may be used easily to control outdoor pests. Ladybugs will attack aphids; green lacewings will eat aphids, mealy grubs, whiteflies, mites, and thrips' eggs and larvae; spined soldier bugs will eat large caterpillars; and praying mantises will help control a variety of pesky insects. Beneficial insects and instructions on their proper care and usage can be ordered from any of the suppliers listed in the resources.

Companion Plantings If you want to avoid pests in the garden without resorting to chemical sprays or lots of work, try companion planting. Grow insect-repelling flowers and herbs in your garden, such as marigolds and nasturtiums to keep out beetles, whiteflies, and nematodes; spearmint to keep ants at bay; geraniums to repel Japanese beetles; garlic and chives to help fight aphids, Japanese beetles, and weevils. Rosemary makes life miserable for cabbage moths; borage keeps hornworms from chewing up your tomatoes; and tansy or pennyroyal work as general all-around repellants. Other types of flowers attract birds that eat insects. Since some plants seem to be natural bug repellants and some plants seem to attract them, inter-planting the repellants between the rows of vegetables and herbs that attract nuisance bugs will work as a fairly effective and natural pesticide. If you don't know which plants to use, contact your local nursery or one of the several resources listed on page 168.

Mosquito Repellant Take 500 to 1,000 units of Vitamin B1 orally ½ to 1 hour before going out. Its efficacy lasts for several hours.

Wasp repellant There isn't one. And those stings hurt! The best idea is to avoid them. I remember my daughter howling when, at age six, she was stung by a really angry one! I used my grandmother's recipe of oatmeal and baking soda mixed with a little water to make a paste. When I applied it to my daughter's sting, it immediately eased the pain.

ECOLOGICAL CLEANING RESOURCES

Arm & Hammer Use Wheel Offer
P.O. Box 7285
Monticello, MN 55563-7285
www.armandhammer.com
Cleaning booklet for using baking soda

Annie Berthold-Bond
www.anniebbond.com
Check her Web site, and ask your local
book dealer to order a copy of *Clean and
Green: The Complete Guide to Nontoxic
and Environmentally Safe Housekeeping*
and *Better Basics for the Home*, or check
your local library

Beverly De Julio
Box 111
Palatine, IL 60078
www.handymaam.tv
Environmentally safe cleaning

Gaiam Living, Inc.
www.gaiamlife.com
Environmentally safe wood floor wax,
organic cotton bedding and clothing, etc.

Greenpeace
1436 U Street N.W.
Washington, D.C. 20009
(202) 462-1177
www.greenpeace.org
Cleaning and pesticide information

GreenPeople
www.greenpeople.org
Tons of environmental information

Women's Voices for the Earth
www.womenandenvironment.org
Provides online information about
cleaning products, and the article
"Disinfectant Overkill: How Too Clean
May Be Hazardous to Our Health"

3M Company
(800) 338-FILTER
www.3m.com
Safer furniture stripping and refinishing
products and filters for furnaces and
air conditioners may be purchased at
your local hardware store, or call 3M's
consumer relations number, above, for
more information

20 Mule Team Borax
Dial Corp., a Henkel Company
15101 N. Scottsdale Rd. MS 5028
Scottsdale, AZ 85254
(800) 528-0849
www.20muleteamlaundry.com
Free cleaning information available

ORGANIC HERBICIDE AND PESTICIDE SUPPLIERS AND ORGANIZATIONS

Arbico Organics
(800) 827-2847
www.arbico-organics.com
Organic pesticides and other supplies

Beneficial Insectary
(800) 477-3715
www.insectary.com
Beneficial insects for order

Bozeman Bio-Tech
P.O. Box 3146
Bozeman, MT 59772
(800) 289-6656
Free catalog and consulting for organic
pesticides and other supplies

Buglogical Control Systems, Inc.
(520) 298-4400
www.buglogical.com
Organic solutions to pest control problems

Consumer Reports
www.consumerreports.org
Food additive and other information, with
a search function and short descriptions;
detailed information requires subscription

Gardens Alive!
5100 Schenley Place
Lawrenceburg, IN 47025
(513) 354-1482
www.gardensalive.com
Beneficial insects, Sunspray UltraFine
Spray Oil, and environmentally responsible
gardening products

Garden Ville
6266 Hwy. 290 West
Austin, TX 78735
(512) 892-0006
www.garden-ville.com
Beneficial insects and online Ask
the Expert feature

**National Center for
Environmental Health Strategies**
1100 Rural Ave.
Voorhees, NJ 08043
(856) 429-5358
www.ncehs.org

Beyond Pesticides
701 E Street S.E.
Washington, DC 20003
www.beyondpesticides.org

Nature's Control
3960 W. Main St.
Medford, OR 97501
(541) 245-6033
www.naturescontrol.com
Beneficial insects

W. Atlee Burpee & Co.
300 Park Ave.
Warminster, PA 18974
(800) 333-5808
www.burpee.com
Beneficial insects and
other gardening supplies

Resources

Many cities and towns do not have conveniently located health food stores, and your local supermarket may not carry grains, flours, and other baking ingredients suitable for your child. We have contacted each of the manufacturers and sellers listed below to verify that they will ship to individuals or to buying clubs, or provide information about local distributors. All will charge shipping and handling costs. Buying in bulk, however, will limit the money you have to spend on those charges. We store our grains and flours in airtight plastic containers or glass jars, which eliminate any possible bug problem and allow us to purchase and store much more than just one pound at a time. Just remember to label your containers immediately. Many of the gluten and nongluten flours look very similar to one another. Also, if you feel you will not use up the flours within two months, store them in air-tight containers in the freezer to prevent souring. Baked breads are best stored in ziplock bags in the freezer immediately after purchasing them.

You might also want to check with your accountant or tax preparer to see if any of the special ingredients, foods, and allergy products you must buy for your allergic child, and any of the attendant costs, such as specialty cookbooks and shipping charges, are tax-deductible as a medical expense. A general rule of thumb is that if your doctor has prescribed special products, including foods, for your allergic child because of an elimination diet, you may deduct the cost of the foods that exceed the cost of the nonallergenic foods; for example, if your doctor has prescribed wheat- and corn-free products and a loaf of white bread is available at the supermarket for $2.89 a loaf while a loaf of rice bread of the same size costs $4.50, you may deduct $1.61, the difference between what you would have paid for the white bread and what you must now pay for the spelt bread.

Manufacturers and suppliers are listed alphabetically, followed by allergy control products, allergy and asthma support organizations, and cookbooks we found helpful.

INGREDIENTS MANUFACTURERS AND SUPPLIERS

Arrowhead Mills, Inc.
(866) 595-8917
www.arrowheadmills.com
Flours, mixes, gluten-free products, grains, beans, and seeds; nut and seed butters; oils; breakfast cereals

Bob's Red Mill Natural Foods, Inc.
www.bobsredmill.com
Flours, mixes; recipes

Bremner Food Group, Inc.
www.bremnerbiscuit.com
Ry Krisp crackers, etc.

Cook's Vanilla
www.cooksvanilla.com
Gluten-free and alcohol-free vanillas

Dakota Prairie Organic Flour Co.
500 North Street West
Harvey, ND 58341
(701) 324-4330
www.dakota-prairie.com
Gluten-free and wheat-free flours; find distributors on the Web site

Diamond Organics
1272 Highway 1
Moss Landing, CA 95039
(888) ORGANIC
www.diamondorganics.com
Provides organically grown foods to customers nationwide by direct home delivery

Dietary Specialties
8 S. Commons Rd.
Waterbury, CT 06704
(888) 640-2800
www.dietspec.com
Cake and bread mixes, cookies and crackers, cereals, gluten-free products, pastas, flours, baking products

Earth Balance Foods
www.earthbalancenatural.com
Vegan shortening, natural and organic foods; contact online for a list of retailers in your area

Eden Foods, Inc.
701 Tecumseh Rd.
Clinton, MI 49236
(800) 424-3336
www.edenfoods.com
Soy milk products, grains, canned goods; contact for a list of retailers in your area; Eden Foods does not sell to individual consumers

Ener-G Foods, Inc.
P.O. Box 84487
Seattle, WA 98124-5787
(800) 331-5222
www.ener-g.com
Ener-G Egg Replacer powder, flours, grains, breads, mixes and ready-to-make foods, pastas, nondairy beverages, low-protein and gluten-free products, and recipes

Enjoy Life Foods
www.enjoylifefoods.com
Gluten-free, dairy-free chocolate chips;
cookies; snacks; see Web site for local
distributors

Frontier Natural Products Coop
www.frontiercoop.com
Alcohol-free vanillas, organic spices
and blends, other baking and cooking
ingredients, and seasonings; see Web site
for local distributors

Gluten Free Oats, LLC
www.glutenfreeoats.com
(888) 941-9922
Varieties of gluten-free oats and recipes

Gold Mine Natural Food Company
7805 Arjons Dr.
San Diego, CA 92126-4368
(800) 475-3663
www.goldminenaturalfood.com
Certified natural, organic, and kosher
products; grains and beans; snacks; flours;
household and personal products

Grainaissance, Inc.
1580 62nd St.
Emeryville, CA 94608
(800) 472-4697
www.grainaissance.com
Organic, kosher, plain and flavored rice
milks, rice pudding, and ready-to-bake
rice doughs; contact online for retailers in
your area

Hain *and* Health Valley Foods, Inc.
(866) 595-8917
www.healthvalley.com
Hain Baking Powder (cereal-free), Health
Valley soups, pastas, prepared foods,
soy milk, cookies and crackers, cereals;
contact for retailers in your area

Jackson Mitchell
Meyenberg Goat Milk Products
P.O. Box 934
Turlock, CA 95381
(800) 891-GOAT
www.meyenberg.com
Organic goat's milk products, recipes;
contact for local retailers

Jaffe Bros. Inc.
28560 Lilac Rd.
Valley Center, CA 92082
(877) 975-2333
www.organicfruitsandnuts.com
Organic dried fruits, nuts, and butters;
beans; grains; flours; pastas; raw agave
nectar

Land o' Lakes, Inc.
www.landolakes.com
A recommended combination of flours
for a gluten-free flour mixture to make
and keep at home; see Web site for
directions

Natural Lifestyle Supplies
16 Lookout Dr.
Asheville, NC 28804-3330
(828) 254-9606
www.natural-lifestyle.com
Flours, grains, and baking ingredients; cereals, beans, and seeds; pastas; herbs, seasonings, and sea salts; rice and soy milks; household and personal items

Selina Naturally
www.selinanaturally.com
(800) 867-7258
Celtic sea salt

Timber Creek Farms
P.O. Box 606
Yorkville, IL 60560
(630) 553-1119
www.timbercreekorganics.com
Certified organic produce, juices, and meats; grains and nuts; some flours

Wilderness Family
www.wildernessfamilynaturals.com
Coconut products; information about coconut flour, oil, etc.

ALLERGY CONTROL PRODUCTS

Allergy Control Products, Inc.
22 Shelter Rock Lane
Danbury, CT 06810
(800) ALLERGY
www.allergycontrol.com
Mattress covers, pillowcases, blankets, air cleaners, carpet sprays, furnace filters, respiratory care products; blog; 24/7 Ask an Expert at above number

ORGANIZATIONS

Allernet
www.allernet.com
Provides up-to-date information
regarding allergies and asthma, sponsored
by the National Pollen Network

**American Academy of Allergy,
Asthma & Immunology**
85 W. Algonquin Rd.
Suite 550
Arlington Heights, IL 60005
(847) 427-1200
www.aaaaci.org
Provides information about allergies and
works to improve the quality of patient
care; see Web site for tapes and brochures

**American Dietetic Association's
Consumer Nutrition Hotline**
(800) 877-1600 x4844
www.eatright.org
Answers to your food and nutrition
questions, or a referral to a registered
dietitian in your area

American Lung Association
www.lungusa.org
See Web site for asthma information and
nearest chapter

**Asthma and Allergy Foundation
of America**
(800) 7-ASTHMA
www.aafa.org
Provides information about asthma and
allergies

Celiac Sprue Association
P.O. Box 31700
Omaha, NE 68131-0700
(877) CSA-4CSA
www.csaceliacs.org
Provides information, updates, and
recipes for gluten-free and wheat-free
diets

Food Allergy and Anaphylaxis Network
11781 Lee Jackson Hwy.
Suite 160
Fairfax, VA 22030-3309
(800) 929-4040
www.foodallergy.org
Updates, political action news, e-mail
newsletter with recipes, dietitian's
column, product updates, allergy
research, and medication information;
$30.00 annual membership fee

Food-Allergy.Org
www.food-allergy.org
Provides information on books and
resources, including gluten-free resources

**Gluten Intolerance Group
of North America**
31214 124th Ave. SE
Auburn, WA 98092-3667
(253) 833-6655
www.gluten.net
Product information, food services and
recipes, events and programs for gluten-
free and wheat-free diets

**National Allergy and Asthma Network/
Mothers of Asthmatics**
2751 Prosperity Ave.
Suite 150
Fairfax, VA 22031
(800) 878-4403
www.aanma.org
Information packets and books on
asthma and allergies (some in Spanish),
and videos for children

**National Jewish Health for
Immunology and Respiratory Medicine**
(800) 222-LUNG
www.nationaljewish.org
Indoor air testing kits, literature on
asthma and other respiratory illnesses;
Find a Doctor and Ask a Nurse resources

**Physicians Committee for Responsible
Medicine**
(202) 686-2210
www.pcrm.org
Information and alerts on allergies and
other medical conditions; e-mail updates

ON-LINE SUPPORT GROUPS AND NEWSLETTERS

www.allergicchild.com
Free monthly newsletter with food, recipes, and political information

www.allergykids.com
Information about products, classroom guides, and safe school programs, other resources

**Eat, Learn, Live/
The ELL Foundation, Inc.**
www.ellfoundation.org
Information about meal and party planning; ingredients mislabeling information and government standards alerts; allergy-free recipes; products for sale

www.indigorabbit.com
Information about foods and alerts, and blogs by mother and son; affiliated Web site www.rainbowonyourplate.com provides information about foods that can be ordered

**Food Allergy Associate of
Wisconsin, Inc. (FAAW)**
www.foodallergywis.org
Support group with online information, meetings, and lending library

Mothers of Children Having Allergies (MOCHA)
www.mochallergies.org
Support and resources for families dealing with food and other types of allergies

Protect Allergic Kids
www.protectallergickids.com
Focuses on eosinophilic esophagitis

Raising Food Allergic Kids (RFAK)
www.rfak.org
Information alerts, book reviews, and a mom's blog

COOKBOOKS

Baking for Health, Linda Edwards (Avery Publishing Group, Inc., $8.95)

Cooking for the Allergic Child, Judy Moyer (Grove Printing, $19.95)

Dr. Mandell's Allergy-Free Cookbook, Fran Gare Mandell (Simon & Schuster, out of print; look for used copies online or check local libraries)

Gluten-Free Baking Classics, Annalise G. Roberts (Agate Surrey, $12.21)

More from the Gluten-Free Gourmet, Bette Hagman (Henry Holt, $25.00)

Quaker Oat Bran Favorite Recipes, Quaker Oats Company (Quaker Oats Company, $3.50)

The Allergy Cookbook and Food Buying Guide, Pamela Nonken and S. Roger Hirsch, M.D. (Warner Brother Books, out of print; look for used copies online or check local libraries)

The Allergy Survival Guide and Cookbook: To Your Good Health!, Carolyn Stone and Jan Beima (CC & Co., out of print; look for used copies online or check local libraries)

Appendix I

COMMON, SCIENTIFIC, AND FAMILY NAMES

COMMON NAME	SCIENTIFIC NAME	FAMILY NAME
Amaranth	*Amaranthus*	Amaranthaceae; Amaranth Family
Arrowroot	*Maranta arundinacea*	Marantaceae; Arrowroot Family
Barley	*Hordeum*	Poaceae; Grass Family
Buckwheat	*Fagopyrum esculentum*	Polygonaceae; Buckwheat Family
Chickpea or Garbanzo	*Cicer arietinum*	Fabaceae; Bean Family
Coconut	*Cocos nucifera*	Arecaceae; Palm Family
Kamut	*Triticum*	Poaceae; Grass Family
Millet	*Pennisetum americanum*	Poaceae; Grass Family
Oat	*Avena sativa*	Poaceae; Grass Family
Potato	*Solanum tuberosum*	Solanaceae; Potato Family
Quinoa	*Chenopodium quinoa*	Chenopodiaceae; Goosefoot Family
Rice	*Oryza sativa*	Poaceae; Grass Family
Rye	*Secale cereale*	Poaceae; Grass Family
Soy	*Glycine max*	Fabaceae; Bean Family
Spelt	*Triticum aestivum*	Poaceae; Grass Family
Teff	*Eragrostis ref*	Poaceae; Grass Family
Wheat	*Triticum*	Poaceae; Grass Family

Courtesy of Dr. David G. Fisher

Appendix II

FOOD FAMILIES

Following is a list of common Family names; under each name is a list of the fruits, vegetables, nuts, or grains that belong in that Family. This is not a complete list, but it reflects most of the ingredients used in this cookbook.

Agar Family
  yeast

Amaranth Family
  amaranth

Amaryllis Family
  aquamil

Apple Family
  apples (including cider and vinegar)
  pears
  quinces

Arrowroot Family
  arrowroot

Banana Family
  bananas
  plantains

Bean or Legume Family
  carob
  chickpeas or garbanzo beans
  kudzu or kudu
  licorice
  peanuts
  soy (including soy flour, soy sauce, and tofu)

Birch Family
  filberts
  hazelnuts

Buckwheat Family
  buckwheat
  rhubarb
  sorrel

Cashew Family
  cashews
  mangos
  pistachios

Citrus Family
  grapefruits
  lemons
  limes
  oranges
  tangerines

Composite Family
  safflower (and safflower oil)
  sunflower (and sunflower oil)

Ginger Family
    cardamom
    ginger
    turmeric

Gooseberry Family
    currants
    gooseberries

Goosefoot Family
    beets (and beet sugar)
    quinoa

Grape Family
    cream of tartar
    grapes (including brandy, raisins,
    some regular and balsamic vinegars,
    and most wines)

Grass Family (Cereal and Grain)
    barley (and barley malt)
    cane sugar (including brown sugar,
    molasses, and turbinado)
    corn
    kamut
    millet
    oat
    rice
    rye
    spelt
    teff
    wheat

Heather Family
    blueberries
    cranberries
    huckleberries
    wintergreen

Laurel Family
    cinnamon
    sassafras

Honey Family
    honey

Legume Family, See Bean or Legume Family

Madder Family
    coffee

Macadamia Family
    macadamias

Maple Family
    maple (including maple sugar
    and maple syrup)

Mulberry Family
    breadfruit
    figs
    mulberries

Myrtle Family
    allspice
    cloves

Nutmeg Family
    mace
    nutmeg

Olive Family
    olives (including green and black
    olives and olive oil)

Orchid Family
    vanilla

Palm Family
   coconuts
   dates

Pineapple Family
   pineapples

Plum Family
   almonds
   apricots
   cherries
   nectarines
   peaches
   plums (including prunes)

Potato Family
   white and yellow potatoes

Rose Family
   blackberries
   boysenberries
   loganberries
   raspberries
   strawberries

Sesame Family
   sesame (including oil, seeds,
   and tahini)

Spurge Family
   tapioca

Sterculia Family
   cocoa
   cola

Sweet Potato Family
   sweet potatoes

Triticum Family
   kamut
   spelt
   wheat

Walnut Family
   black walnuts
   English walnuts
   hickory nuts
   pecans

Food families are groups of foods with common botanical attributes based on flower and genetic structures. A person with an allergy to one member of a specific food family may also be allergic to other foods in the same family. If your child is allergic to one food in a particular family, check with your doctor before using other members of that food family.

Dr. Mandell's Allergy-Free Cookbook, Fran Gare Mandell, 1981.

The Allergy Survival Guide and Cookbook: To Your Good Health! Carolyn Stone and Jan Beima, 1988.

Index

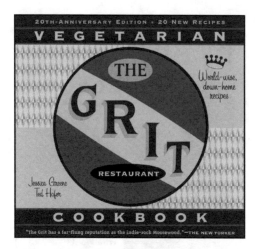

The Grit Cookbook
World-Wise, Down-Home Recipes
JESSICA GREENE and **TED HAFER**

978-1-55652-648-0
$18.95 (CAN $20.95)

"The Grit has a far-flung reputation as the indie-rock Moosewood." —*The New Yorker*

"A legendary vegetarian eatery."
—*Travel & Leisure*

"The Grit is a great restaurant. They have consummate taste." **—Michael Stipe**

"A hip eatery that lets you fill up without emptying your pockets. Tempting vegetarian fare that even the most devout carnivores come to crave." **—CNN.com**

"The Grit serves split pea soup every day of the week and, even better, it's curried pea soup. What a unique idea! What a surprising taste treat." **—Spaulding Gray**

"Whenever I visit my old stomping grounds in Athens, my first stop is always The Grit!"
—Kate Pierson, The B-52's

"If every town had a vegetarian restaurant as good as The Grit, there would be a lot more cows, pigs, and chickens running around."
—Dave School, Widespread Panic

"I can hardly count the number of times The Grit has saved my life: perfect vittles in a wasteland of scary tour food."

—Kristin Hersh

The Grit, in the quintessential boho town of Athens, Georgia, is known far and wide as the touring musicians' restaurant of choice. True to its Southern roots, the menu at this hip vegetarian eatery combines soul-food sensibility with meatless cuisine. While there are plenty of Italian, Indian, Mexican, and Middle-Eastern favorites to satisfy the well-traveled vegetarian, the heart of this cuisine maintains the down-home, soul-food feeling of simple foods and classic combinations guaranteed to please. This classic cookbook features 150 of The Grit's most requested recipes including 20 new recipes, 20 savory, and 20 sweet, to celebrate the 20th anniversary of this famous establishment.

CHICAGO REVIEW PRESS

Available at your favorite bookstore, (800) 888-4741, or www.chicagoreviewpress.com

By Any Greens Necessary

A Revolutionary Guide for Black Women Who Want to Eat Great, Get Healthy, Lose Weight, and Look Phat

TRACYE LYNN McQUIRTER, MPH

978-1-55652-998-6
$14.95 (CAN $16.95)

- More than 40 delicious and nutritious recipes highlighted with color photographs
- Menus and advice on transitioning from omnivore to vegan
- Resource information and a comprehensive shopping list for restocking the fridge and pantry

African American women are facing a health crisis: Heart disease, stroke, and diabetes occur more frequently among them than among women of other races. Black women comprise the heftiest group in the nation—80 percent are overweight and 50 percent obese. Decades of studies show that these chronic diseases can be prevented and even reversed with a plant-based diet. But how can you control your weight and health without sacrificing great food and gorgeous curves?

With attitude, inspiration, and expertise McQuirter shows women how to stay healthy, hippy, and happy by eating plenty of fresh fruits and vegetables, whole grains, and legumes as part of an active lifestyle. The book is a call to action that all women should heed.